SEXUAL POLITICS AND THE EUROPEAN UNION

The New Feminist Challenge

SEXUAL POLITICS AND THE EUROPEAN UNION

The New Feminist Challenge

Edited by

R. AMY ELMAN

Berghahn Books
Providence • Oxford

Published in 1996 by

Berghahn Books
Editorial offices:
165 Taber Avenue, Providence, RI 02906, USA
Bush House, Merewood Avenue, Oxford, OX3 8EF, UK

Library of Congress Cataloging-in-Publication Data
Sexual politics and the European Union : the new feminist challenge /
    edited by R. Amy Elman
        p.   cm.
    Revisions of papers presented at a May 1994 conference sponsored
by the Center for European Studies, Kalamazoo College in conjunction
with the International Area Studies and Women's Studies Programs.
    Includes bibliographical references.
    ISBN 1-57181-062-5 (alk. paper). -- ISBN 1-57181-046-3 (alk.
paper)
    1. Women--European Union countries--Social conditions--Congresses.
2. Women's rights--European Union countries--Congresses. 3. Women-
-Legal status, laws, etc.--European Union countries--Congresses.
4. Feminism--European Union countries--Congresses. I. Elman, R.
Amy, 1961–   .
HQ1587.S49   1996   95-43215
305.42'094--dc20   CIP

British Library Cataloguing in Publication Data
A CIP catalogue record for this book is available from
the British Library.

Printed in the United States on acid-free paper

CONTENTS

PREFACE   vii

ABBREVIATIONS   viii

INTRODUCTION: THE EU FROM FEMINIST   1
PERSPECTIVES
R. Amy Elman

1. THE EUROPEAN UNION AND THE WOMEN WITHIN: 13
   AN OVERVIEW OF WOMEN'S RIGHTS POLICY
   Catherine Hoskyns

2. EUROPEAN UNION SEXUAL HARASSMENT POLICY   23
   Evelyn Collins

3. THE INTERPLAY: THE FORMATION OF SEXUAL   35
   HARASSMENT LEGISLATION IN FRANCE AND
   EU POLICY INITIATIVES
   Amy G. Mazur

4. PORNOGRAPHY AND SEXUAL HARASSMENT   51
   IN THE EU
   Susanne Baer

5. PORNOGRAPHY, HARM, AND HUMAN RIGHTS: 67
   THE UK IN EUROPEAN CONTEXT
   Catherine Itzin

6. SEXUAL TRAFFICKING OF WOMEN IN EUROPE: 83
   A HUMAN RIGHTS CRISIS FOR THE
   EUROPEAN UNION
   Dorchen Leidholdt

7. REPRODUCTIVE TECHNOLOGIES IN GERMANY: 97
   AN ISSUE FOR THE EUROPEAN UNION
   Ute Winkler

8. "AND NOBODY WAS ANY THE WISER": 109
   IRISH ABORTION RIGHTS AND THE
   EUROPEAN UNION
   Ailbhe Smyth

9. THE COMMON MARKET OF VIOLENCE 131
   Jalna Hanmer

10. THE EUROPEAN UNION AND THE 147
    FUTURE OF FEMINISM
    Christine Delphy

REFERENCES 159

NOTES ON CONTRIBUTORS 170

INDEX 173

PREFACE

The essays in this volume were first presented at "Women, The European State, and Community," an international conference sponsored by the Center for European Studies at Kalamazoo College in conjunction with the International Area Studies and Women's Studies Programs (May 1994). The meeting proved extraordinary because of the collection of those women who chose to participate. Each presentation was revised for this volume and also takes into account developments since the conference.

I would like to thank those students and colleagues who assisted in planning the conference. Special appreciation is extended to the Center for European Studies at New York University where, as a visiting scholar, I was able to edit this volume. Lastly, there are several individuals whose generous support throughout this work must be noted: David Barclay, Nora Evers, Gail Griffin, Annie McCombs, Janet Riley, Florence Rush, Elizabeth Salkind, and Martin Schain.

ABBREVIATIONS

AVFT	Association Européenne Contre Les Violences Faites aux Femmes au Travail (a French Association Against Violence Against Women at Work)
BSC	Broadcasting Standards Council (Britain)
CADAC	Coordination nationale des Associations pour le Droit à l'Avortement et à la Contraception (The National Coordination for the Right to Abortion and Contraception in France)
CAT	Convention Against Torture and Other Cruel, Inhumane or Degrading Treatment or Punishment
CEDAW	Convention on the Elimination of All Forms of Discrimination Against Women
CFDT	Confédération Française Démocratique du Travail (one of five French labor organizations)
CHSCT	Comité d'Hygiène de Sécurité et des Conditions de Travail (Work Place Health & Safety Committee in France)
CMLR	Common Market Law Reports
CRC	Convention on the Rights of the Child
CSEP	Conseil Supérieur de l'Egalité Professionelle (France's High Council for Equal Employment)
CVF	Chronic Villi Sampling
Dir.	Directive
DMWR	Deputy Minister of Women's Rights (France)
Doc.	Document
EC	European Community
ECHR	European Convention on Human Rights

ECHR	European Court on Human Rights (European Council)
ECJ	European Court of Justice
ECR	European Court Reports (Reports of the Court of Justice of the European Communities, Luxembourg)
ECSC	European Coal and Steel Community (France, West Germany, Italy, BENELUX)
ECU	European Currency Unit
EEC	European Economic Community
EHRR	European Human Rights Reports (European Council)
EMU	Economic and Monetary Union
ENWRAC	European Network for Women's Rights to Abortion and Contraception
EOC	Equal Opportunities Commission (Britain)
EP	European Parliament
EU	European Union
ICCPR	International Covenant on Civil and Political Rights
ICERD	International Convention on the Elimination of All Forms of Racial Discrimination
ICESCR	International Covenant on Economic, Social, and Cultural Rights
ILO	International Labour Organization
INTERPOL	International Crime Police Organization
IRLR	International Relations Law Reports
IVF	In Vitro Fertilization
IWLM	Irish Women's Liberation Movement
LDF	Ligue du Droit des Femme (The League of Women's Rights, France)
MEP	Member of European Parliament
MLF	Mouvement de Libération des Femmes (the French Women's Liberation Movement)

MP	Member of Parliament
NAWO	National Alliance of Women's Organizations (Britain)
NGO	Non-governmental organizations (United Nations)
OECD	Organization for Economic Cooperation and Development
OFW	Office of Women's Rights (France)
OJ	Official Journal of the European Community
SEA	Single European Act (1986)
TEU	Treaty on European Union (also known as the Maastricht Treaty 1992)
UK	United Kingdom
UN	United Nations
WASH	Women Against Sexual Harassment (Britain)

INTRODUCTION
The EU from Feminist Perspectives

R. Amy Elman

The politics of European integration is rarely discussed in a manner which holds the sexual subordination of women as political in nature, economic in consequence, and worthy of state or Union action. In those few instances where women's issues take precedence, the focus has been on employment or gender inequality, to the exclusion of the political implications of sexual abuse and male violence. This volume attempts to change this and, consequently, contribute to a more comprehensive assessment and innovative approach to women and the European Union (EU).[1]

There is a reason that the European Union's capacity for and commitment to women's equality (and general well-being) is consistently discussed and approached within an economic context: the unification of Europe is primarily an economically inspired plan. Consequently, considerations of sexual (in)equality have been informed by this context. Indeed, the founding constitution of the European Community, the 1957 Treaty of Rome, stipulated in Article 119 that Member States should apply the principle of sexual equality through "equal pay for equal work." While this principle is clearly meritorious, gender inequality persists both within and outside of European wage labor markets. Moreover, the economic situation of women in Europe has been deteriorating (United Nations

---

1. In their ground-breaking volume on women's rights in the European Community, Mary Buckley and Malcolm Anderson explain that issues like violence against women and the traffic in women are "problems with low political salience and therefore remain neglected" (1988, 12). They note the need for a second volume on women and the European Community, one which could "provide a more exhaustive assessment of the lives of women in Europe" (1988, 17). It is my hope that this volume is a step in that direction.

Information Service, 28 September 1994). This suggests that economic palliatives, while necessary, are insufficient in ending women's subordination—economic and otherwise.[2]

Even as the European Union has attempted to address economic discrimination, additional issues of women's rights and inequality are becoming increasingly difficult to ignore. Indeed, the economic focus of the EU agenda cannot render issues such as abortion, battery, rape, and pornography extraneous or inconsequential. To the contrary, one of the fundamental insights of feminism is the understanding that so-called private issues are, at once, personal, political, and economic. Throughout her analysis of the Union's established women's policy in Chapter 1, Catherine Hoskyns demonstrates that the artificial divisions between public and private (social and economic) "have proved as hard to maintain in policy as in real life."

This collection of essays provides a unique exploration of the ways in which EU policies and actions affect more than just the realm of employment—they significantly influence the everyday lives of women. The authors examine sexual harassment, woman battery, pornography, sexual trafficking, abortion, and reproductive technologies within a context generally perceived as excluding such issues. By extending an explicitly political analysis to these matters, the contributors are able to surpass a purely economic and more conventional conception of rights, conflicts, and interests within the European Union.

This level of inquiry is as innovative as it is necessary. Indeed, many EU commentators who relied on traditional notions of politics were incredulous and unable to explain how the rape of a fourteen-year-old Irish girl ("X") and her subsequent desire for an abortion could give pause to the seemingly assured process of European integration. This is one example among many which clearly underscores the need for a deeper understanding of the relationship of sexual politics to European integration.

As scholars, we face an important challenge. If our work is to be evaluated continuously against the standard of its capacity to understand political reality, we must realize that our scholarship risks inadequacy unless we acknowledge fully that sexuality informs our conceptions of rights, interests, and oppression. An examination of sexual inequality that fails to implicate sexuality is not only inexact;

---

2. Susanne Baer provides an alternative explanation (Chapter 4). She asserts that conceptions of "equality" are fundamentally flawed both within and outside of Community law.

it leaves a central component of women's subordination unexplored and intact.[3] Sexuality, as we will see from these essays, is profoundly political. It is socially constructed as opposed to a force over which we have no control; for women in particular, sexuality is often regulated and commodified. The numerous ways in which the European Union is involved or (selectively) indifferent to this complex process unite this otherwise diverse collection of essays, which range widely in terms of theme, country, and discipline.

This collection is not intended to establish a survey of the European Union, its institutions, and Member States. Instead, the contributors either focus on the EU more generally or address the generalities that can be derived from particular case studies. This anthology is thus intended to provide a foundation upon which one can begin to assess the politics of European integration from a feminist perspective.[4] In doing this, it fundamentally alters the discursive terrain of the EU and the politics of integration. Yet, before venturing on this alternate path, it is vital to establish a common framework from which to proceed. The following overview of the EU, its origins and institutions, is written for this purpose.

The European Union: Origins

The European Union has its roots in the French-inspired European Coal and Steel Community (ECSC), founded in 1952.[5] The six original constituent nations (Belgium, France, Germany, Italy, Luxembourg, and the Netherlands) pledged to consolidate their coal and steel resources by providing a common market for these products and by agreeing to supranational management and a

---

3. Failure to analyze critically sexuality may also represent a cowardice to challenge the very foundation upon which women's subordination is maintained. In an age which appears to affirm obscurity, it is easy to understand the analytical shift away from a feminist, materialist, and gender-specific analysis of women's oppression to the political neutrality offered by "gendered" analysis. "Identity politics" functions in a similar vein. It is a means of having an analysis of difference without having to address dominance.

4. A "feminist" perspective is one which holds that women are (as a group) oppressed by men. It is a viewpoint that recognizes the injustice of this condition and seeks to change it. Methodologically, feminism places women at the center of analysis and seeks to "extract the truth of women's commonalities out of the lie that all women are the same" (MacKinnon 1983, 639).

5. French foreign minister, Robert Schuman, proposed the plan in 1950. The treaty that established the ECSC is also known as the Schuman Plan.

common system of law. To this end, each member nation lifted restrictions on related imports and exports from the others.

This agreement established a vital precedent for the eventual creation of an enlarged common European market. The appeal of this arrangement was not, however, purely economic. Europe had just emerged from the Second World War. The ECSC can be understood as a Cold War enterprise, a means of bringing a strong, remilitarized and fiscally fit Federal German Republic into the West. A united Europe also seemed to promise the transcendence of those national rivalries and parochial loyalties that helped make the past horrors of that period possible. Indeed, the Preamble to the ECSC explicitly calls upon its members "to substitute for age-old rivalries the merging of their essential interests" and "create, by establishing an economic community, the basis for a broader and deeper community among peoples long divided by bloody conflicts." It was assumed that the eventual prosperity prompted by a cohesive economic community would diminish dissension of all kinds.

Five years later, in March 1957, the six ECSC Member States adopted the Treaty of Rome. This treaty created two additional communities to facilitate a more economically cohesive Europe— the European Atomic Energy Community (Euratom) and the European Economic Community (EEC or Common Market). The former established the common development of Europe's nuclear energy resources;[6] the latter sought a more comprehensive economic and social integration. Unlike the ECSC and Euratom, the European Economic Community's (EEC) interests were not restricted to coal, steel, and energy. In 1962, for example, the EEC adopted a common market for agricultural products. The EEC's objective was to create a single economic region within which capital, goods, services and persons could freely move.

In 1965, the three distinct communities of Europe (ECSC, Euratom, and EEC) signed the Merger Treaty to consolidate their separate goals and institutions. The six founding states were to share membership within a singular European Community and, as was stipulated by the earlier Treaty of Rome, any European state could apply to join them. In 1973, Britain, Denmark, and Ireland entered into this community. Greece joined in 1981. Four years later, Portugal and Spain signed a Treaty of Accession; by 1985 the European Community consisted of twelve nations.

6. Euratom encouraged the coordination of research programs, set safety guidelines and established the free flow of nuclear materials, equipment, and specialists within the Community.

In the same period, the twelve Member States soon strengthened their internal market through the 1986 adoption of the Single European Act (SEA). This Act enhanced cooperation in foreign policy and called for the removal of border restrictions, differential tariffs, and other trade barriers between the Members by 1992. That year also marked a renewed commitment to the project of a unified Europe through the signing of the Treaty on European Union (TEU), more commonly referred to as the "Maastricht Treaty."

This most ambitious of the European treaties, Maastricht endeavors to create a more cohesive political union through the establishment of a European citizenship, a single European currency (ECU), and a central European bank by 1999.[7] In addition, it sets provisions for a more interventionist European government and strengthened the competencies of the Union to pursue its earlier adopted (SEA) "Social Charter." This charter is a declaration of the rights and principles which operate throughout the Member States. Despite a perceptible trend toward social policy that is less confined to employment-related matters, the EU's "social" regulations generally refer to working conditions (e.g., social security and occupational health and safety).[8] Thus, the term "social" can be somewhat misleading. Moreover, many critics (most notably those from within the European Parliament) have noted that workers' "rights" are not sufficiently clear in intent or practice. Most of the policies explicitly pertaining to women are contained in Social Action Programs.[9] Like other social initiatives, these policies are frequently adopted to improve and grant greater legitimacy to the new, liberal economic order (Majone 1993).

It was only after the Maastricht Treaty had come into force in 1993 that the European Community became more commonly known

7. Under Maastricht, countries must have deficits below three percent of GDP and outstanding public debts below sixty percent of GDP to be eligible to join the single currency. As of 1994, Luxembourg was the only one of the twelve Member States that could meet this dual-pronged requirement. The Organization for Economic Cooperation and Development (OECD) predicts that only five of the current fifteen Member States are likely to meet the deficit target by 1996. Consequently, the future of the Economic and Monetary Union (EMU) remains uncertain (*Financial Times*, 17 January 1995).

8. Of the twenty regulations/directives that implement the Social Charter, half cover occupational health and safety, three concern improvements in living and working conditions and three concern equal treatment for women and men, disabled persons, and child welfare (Majone 1993, 155).

9. These Action Programs will be detailed later in this volume (see especially Collins, Chapter 2).

as the "European Union" (EU). The former is often invoked with reference to the central activities of the European Community prior to this treaty. The "EU" is a more inclusive term, referring to all "European" institutions and initiatives taken since 1993. Still, confusion persists, in part, because any discussion of European integration is inherently dynamic. For example, the membership of the Union was recently enlarged to fifteen when Finland, Sweden, and Austria joined in 1995. A host of other countries are exploring the prospects of membership (e.g., Hungary, Poland, the Czech Republic, Slovakia, and Turkey). Moreover, the Union's ideals, proposals, and institutions have continuously evolved since its inception.[10]

It is to the political institutions of which the EU is comprised that we now turn.[11]

The European Union: Institutions

The Council of Ministers is the primary decision-making body of the European Union and should not be confused with the European Council.[12] The latter consists of the leaders of the Member States who meet semiannually at "summits" to pursue strategic decisions about the Union's future. Such summits usually promote the most visible decisions about European integration. These meetings, in turn, encourage the Council of Ministers and other EU institutions "to work more expeditiously in preparing proposals that ... contribute to the creation of a single [European market]" (Cameron 1992, 64).

10. Upon presenting his plan for the first European community (i.e., the ECSC), Robert Schuman stated: "Europe will not be made at once or according to a single overall plan. It will be built through concrete achievements which first create de facto solidarity" (in Pryce 1987, 46).

11. For a more thorough investigation of the institutions of the European Union, there are numerous volumes. Two of the most comprehensive and interesting are *The European Community and the Challenge of the Future* (Lodge 1993), and *Euro-Politics: Institutions and Policy-Making in the "New" European Community* (Sbragia 1992). Sbragia's collection is particularly adept at explaining the limitations of using analogies between EU and U.S. institutional structures.

12. Moreover, neither the Council of Ministers nor the European Council should be confused with the Council of Europe. The Council of Europe is Europe's oldest pan-European institution. Founded in 1949, it is comprised of over thirty nations. Unlike the EU, its principal aim is the promotion of parliamentary democracy and human rights throughout Europe as affirmed in its European Convention on Human Rights (ECHR). The case law generated by the Council's Court of Human Rights (also ECHR) is influential for the EU's Court of Justice.

The Council of Ministers generally meets in Brussels and is composed of fifteen appointed delegates, one from each Member State. Each delegate chairs the Council for six months on a strictly alphabetical rotation. The Council's decisions are binding and increasingly taken by a qualified majority vote. This body must act on (e.g., accept, amend, or reject) proposals that emanate from the European Commission and (sometimes) the European Parliament.

The European Commission is the institutional embodiment of the EU and is located in Brussels with additional offices in Luxembourg. It consists of twenty commissioners, each of whom are appointed by their Member States for a renewable term of five years.[13] Commissioners are expected to pursue the long-term, *common* interests of the European Union. The Commission proposes public policy and is served by over twenty-two distinct divisions (directorate generals or D-Gs), each of which pursues a particular policy area. Within the Division of Employment, Industrial Relations, and Social Affairs (D-G V), the Equal Opportunities Unit (formerly the Women's Bureau) is charged with the development of women's rights policy. By virtue of its ability to initiate action, the Commission plays a vital role in the Union; however, it is the Council of Ministers that retains the power to reject the proposals from both the Commission and the European Parliament.

The European Parliament (EP) is based in Strasbourg and is comprised of 612 members (MEPs). They are elected directly from their Member States for five-year, renewable terms. The EP is not a typical legislative body; it does not make laws. It is, instead, a body that influences budgetary decisions and elaborates on EU policy directions through power of amendment and veto on select bills. Like the Commission, it too has a permanent advisory body on women's rights (the Women's Rights Committee). Of the four EU institutions, the EP is the most democratic and least powerful. This fact, commonly referred to as "the democratic deficit," compromises the claim that the European Union is informed by the democratic values it professes to promote throughout its Member States. This criticism prompted some adjustments to enhance the Parliament's power. For example, through the Treaty on European Union, the Parliament has been given a limited right of initiative. That is, it can request the Commission to submit proposals on specific matters after it has reached a majority decision. A conference will be held in

---

13. Britain, France, Germany, Italy, and Spain have two commissioners and the remaining ten have one.

1996 to consider how, among other European institutions, the scope of the Parliament's influence can be extended.

The European Court of Justice (ECJ), located in Luxembourg, contains one judge appointed from each Member State for renewable six-year terms. The ECJ functions essentially as a court of appeals for the Union although it can also choose to hear cases—the ECJ takes references from national courts. Member States are expected to ensure the proper implementation of European law and the Court intervenes when this expectation is disappointed. The Court is powerful. Its decisions override those of the Member States and of their courts. The Court interprets and upholds EU legislation, of which there are three kinds: regulations, directives, and recommendations. Regulations are binding in law and are automatically incorporated into the national legal systems. They require no separate ratification. Directives, while also binding, introduce broad objectives and call on Member States to implement them, each in its own way. Recommendations are not binding, but generally function as advice given to governments.

Sexual Politics: European Competence and Will

In considering the "cumbersome mechanics" of the European Union, Ailbhe Smyth remarks on the ensuing alienation people feel from it. "The European Union," she writes, "could not be described as a 'popular' institution, not least because it has made no attempt to appeal to the imagination of its citizens."

One remaining question is whether or not the European Union retains the legal competence, imaginative capacity, and will to pursue the range of women's issues delineated in this volume. None of the founding treaties mentions sexual harassment, pornography, battery, rape, abortion, or reproductive technologies. Indeed, when the Community was first established, most of these issues were deemed so private that they were precluded from the purview of public policy, national and otherwise.[14] The fact that the EU has not remained tacit on these issues testifies to the success feminists have had in politicizing women's sexual subordination.

Throughout this volume, contributors question the ways in which rhetorical commitments to equality can be translated into concrete

---

14. Additionally, the numerous issues raised by reproductive medicine could not be broached because the technologies had not yet been developed.

acts on behalf of women. From its inception, the Community has been reluctant to intervene in the "internal" or "private" affairs of its Member States. Such reticence has been codified recently through the Maastricht requirement of Subsidiarity (Article 3b). Subsidiarity holds that even when it is within the legislative competence of the EU to intervene, such authority should be exercised only if the Union's objectives cannot be sufficiently achieved by Member States themselves. Despite this, the competencies of the EU have expanded and are evolving continuously (Clapham 1993, 249).

In the first chapter, Catherine Hoskyns' discussion of the EU's more established women's policy illustrates how the Community has been persuaded to take action where it has insisted previously it held no authority to do so. In 1971, for example, the European Court of Justice took a restrictive view of the scope of Article 119. Five years later the Court took a more expansive approach to this same Article.[15] Hoskyns credits European women's movements with creating a context within which the Court could be persuaded to reconsider.[16] Consequently, the principle of equal pay for equal work was activated and later enhanced through the adoption of several Equality Directives. These extended the concept of equal pay for equal work to equal pay for work of equal value and legislated for equal treatment in other conditions of employment (e.g., recruitment, training, and dismissal).[17]

Evelyn Collins provides a historical overview of policies and programs pertaining to sexual harassment in employment. Furthermore, she notes that the Equality Directives provided a platform from which the EU could take action in what was for them a new policy area. She concludes, in this second chapter, that the EU's adoption of the Recommendation and Code of Practice (in 1991) precipitated an increased awareness of sexual harassment and enhanced the willingness of Member States to confront the problem. Collins' assertion is substantiated by Amy Mazur's investigation of sexual harassment legislation in France (Chapter 3).

Mazur writes: "Efforts to counter sexual harassment in France are clearly linked to larger EU actions to bring the issue to the public's

15. The Court then boldly asserted that the European Community "is not merely an economic union, but is at the same time intended, by common action, to ensure social progress and seek the constant improvement of living and working conditions of their peoples" (in Clapham 1993, 251).

16. That women's movements articulated the progressive positions for which the EU would later be credited is also noted by Ailbhe Smyth (Chapter 8, note 1).

17. Evelyn Collins elaborates on these Directives in her chapter, "European Union Sexual Harassment Policy" (Chapter 2, note 1).

attention in Member States." She details the significant political and financial contributions of the Community to French reformers. She argues that while the EC compelled action, it did little to influence the content and implementation of sexual harassment legislation. Mazur attributes this gap to the absence of decisive EU policy. After all, the EC adopted a recommendation and not a directive or regulation on the matter. The French law which emerged from this context mirrored the largely symbolic nature of the EU initiative. French legislation thus remains without the authoritative capacity to diminish the incidence of sexual harassment at work. However, Mazur is unwilling to dismiss the EU. She credits it with having encouraged Member States (like France) to pursue controversial policies which they may have otherwise been reluctant to adopt.

Sexual harassment is recognized by the EU as sex discrimination when it happens in the wage labor market but not, as Susanne Baer notes, when it occurs elsewhere or is inherent to the industry—as in the production of pornography. This points to the fact that the EU takes action against sexual discrimination only when it fundamentally hampers production or diminishes profits. "Pornography is recognized as discriminating in the wage labor market but is not recognized as doing harm to women," argues Baer in Chapter 4. The inextricability of sexual harassment from pornography provides a framework through which she examines the deficiencies and incongruities of European law.

With Catherine Itzin's discussion of pornography in Chapter 5, we move from the comparative context provided by Baer into a single case study of the United Kingdom. Like Baer, Itzin notes the conspicuous reluctance of Europe (and, in particular the UK) to address the harms promoted in and through pornography. Moreover, with technological advancements, the pornography industry has expanded in ways that prove resistant to regulation through existing law. For example, pornographers were swift to benefit from a 1989 Directive on Broadcasting (89/552 EEC; OJ L 298/23, 17 October 1989) that stated that any program approved by one Member State is automatically legal in all others. Before this guideline, Britain was able to curtail the importation of much of the pornography freely available in other European countries. Pornographers now have their movies approved by the Netherlands, a Member State notorious for its acceptance of pornography. They then reach their viewers in the UK and other countries by satellite. In less than two years a subscription service called Red Hot Dutch reached 22,000 subscribers across the UK. British pornographer Mark

Garner explains, "I simply saw that there is a lot of money to be made from this [directive] ... Sex sells" (Phillips 1993, 48).

Placed within a larger context, the objective of the EU is the establishment of a common European market for capital, labor, goods, and services. Frequently neglected in EU discussions is the recognition of a devastating fact—women are often sexual commodities on the market rather than laborers within it. In Chapter 6, "Sexual Trafficking of Women in Europe: A Human Rights Crisis for the European Union," Dorchen Leidholdt explores the commodification of women for sex. She provides an overview of the dimensions of the European sex trade. As many as 100,000 women in Europe are existing in conditions of sexual exploitation, most trafficked from non-European countries. The sheer size and scope of this industry has had such far-reaching implications that, as Leidholdt notes, the EU has been forced to address it.

Prostitution provides one context within which to explore the growing commodification of human beings; reproductive technologies yields another. Focusing mostly on Germany, Ute Winkler makes clear that reproductive technologies involve, among other things, the commodification of human life (Chapter 7). Throughout Europe, commercial firms buy and sell "surrogate mothers," sperm, eggs, and embryos. As reproductive technologies gain popularity in some Member States and are prohibited in others, "reproductive tourism" has developed. Winkler points to the costs of inaction and implores a consideration of European initiatives against the patriarchal reproductive establishment—an industry that surreptitiously cloaks itself in the mantel of feminism. Whatever action the EU adopts in the regulation of reproductive "goods and services," the issue of abortion will likely return to the top of the EU agenda. After all, innovations in reproductive technologies also involve a reexamination and continued discussion of when life begins.

Although the European Court of Justice ruled that abortion is a service to which all European citizens are entitled and unification involves a harmonization of laws which would seem to support this, the politics of integration permitted Ireland the autonomy to deny women this right of European citizenship. This was accomplished by Ireland's insertion of a Protocol in the Maastricht Treaty. In her detailed discussion of Irish abortion rights and the European Union (Chapter 8), Ailbhe Smyth reveals the impossible situation faced by the women of Ireland: "in voting against the Treaty, Irish women would be voting against their own best interests, although in point of fact, voting in favor of the Treaty ensured that repressive Irish law overrode the EU in the matter of abortion." Ireland may be unique as the only Member State which still prohibits abortion; but, as Ailbhe Smyth and Ute Winkler remind us, abortion rights are under attack throughout Europe and, indeed, the world.

Women's struggle for self-determination is perhaps most clearly met with the greatest resistance by the men with whom women are most "intimate." Jalna Hanmer's discussion of violence against women in Chapter 9 centers on Britain. It was in this Member State that the issue of woman battering was first politicized in Europe. She notes that, while each Member State has its own story of struggle on this issue, there are many similarities between the states that comprise the EU. For example, all Member States have adopted some basic provisions for women wishing to leave the men who abuse them. However, the EU's approach to "social problems," writes Hanmer, "misses completely the importance of violence against women in maintaining women's social subordination." She argues that such violence must be understood as a barrier to social and economic integration for women. The EU's failure to incorporate action on violence against women in its policies conspicuously undermines its promotion of equal opportunities.

This collection concludes with a gaze into the future. Christine Delphy asserts that the future of feminism in Europe depends mostly on feminists themselves (Chapter 10). Unification from this perspective is less a problem than the ability of feminists throughout the Union to autonomously provide a clear definition of feminism. "European countries are neither so unified nor homogeneous," remarks Delphy. This fact underlines the numerous problems with cross-national scholarship and feminist organizational efforts across Europe. Yet, Delphy argues that the intrinsic difficulties of cross-national dialogue must be openly discussed and researched. One cannot be deterred by complexities; one must move to grasp them. Delphy advances the need for a more coherent, coordinated, and radical feminist movement. Working at the European level will require nothing less. Success at this level can obviate the need for local campaigns within all fifteen Member States, just as losing may obliterate any local victories women have already accrued. The difficulty for feminists is that they lack financial and other resources with which to organize effectively. This places the women of Europe at a particular disadvantage with regard to the politics of integration. Now, more than ever, vigilance is required.

1

THE EUROPEAN UNION AND THE WOMEN WITHIN

An Overview of Women's Rights Policy

Catherine Hoskyns

The policy of the European Union on women's rights has been in operation for more than thirty-five years.[1] It thus sets a framework, hidden but strong, for constructing what it means to be women within the now fifteen Member States. Some women have played a role in developing the policy but women are not yet in a position to control the outcomes. It is possible to bypass, alter, or even break this framework, but in order to do so it is necessary to understand its origins and implications. Given the complexity of EU structures and processes, this is by no means easy.[2]

This article explores the various stages of EU women's rights policy and attempts to enhance our understanding of the complexities associated with European integration. To this end, I have taken a women-centered view, a method that relates policy developments to both feminist theory and different phases of women's activism. Looking at the transnational level makes it easier to see how and on what issues different groups of women are organizing. It also helps to mark the connections between activism and policymaking. In addition, I have asked the question, who profits from women's rights policy and who is disadvantaged by it? Placing women at center stage and viewing the EU from this perspective reveals a

1. The analysis in this article is more fully developed in *Integrating Gender— Women, Law, and Politics in the European Union* (forthcoming, Verso 1996). I am grateful to The Nuffield Foundation for granting me a research fellowship in 1993–1994 and making it possible for me to work on these issues.
2. The European Community became the European Union in 1993 after the coming into force of the Treaty on European Union. In this article I have used European Union when discussing present-day attitudes and events since 1993, and European Community for the earlier periods.

great deal about how the Union has developed and how it operates. Looking at the margins helps define the map.

Women's Rights Policy: Basic Characteristics

Before proceeding with an analysis of the women's policy within the European Union, it is necessary to establish certain basic characteristics that underline it. The first of these is that, formally at least, the women's policy is restricted to dealing with the situation of women in employment. The EU originated as an economic union and the convention has been that it only considers (and regulates) people in their capacity as paid workers. People as citizens remain the responsibility of the Member States.[3] One of the only reasons why there is a policy on women at the Union level is that the increasing labor market activity of women required some adjustment. Yet, dealing with women only in their paid work role reinforces the public/private divide, which, as feminists have demonstrated, constitutes one of the main sources of women's disadvantage. The women's policy excludes from the competence of the EU not only the domestic situations of women, but also issues to do with sexual politics and violence. However, these artificial divisions have proved as hard to maintain in policy as in real life. Consequently, policy developed at the EU level is beginning to transcend the field of employment and influence the domestic and "private" spheres of women's lives.

A second characteristic of the policy is that it is centrally based upon the concept of equality, or equal treatment as the EU prefers to call it. Equal treatment is the basic concept used to construct the common market. Goods, capital, services, and labor originating from the Member States should be subject to the same regulations and "enabled" to circulate freely in the market so that women should become equal to men and be "free" to sell their labor. But for women, the concept of equality, used without supporting positive action or special treatment, is problematic. Do we want to be equal to men? Or do we want compensation for previous disadvantage(s), and an alteration in the general norms and standards upon which equality is based?

3. The Treaty on European Union introduces for the first time the category of "European citizen." Although this concept, at present, is not clearly defined, it is a significant development.

Third, EU policy treats women as a single category. There is very little recognition of the distinctive needs of different groups of women or of their varied positions within society. There is, moreover, no general EU policy concerning either race discrimination or the need for equal treatment between different ethnic groups. This has contributed to the reluctance of EU policymakers to address issues to do with poor women, migrant women, or other groups whose history of marginalization is greater and whose need of redress is more acute. When women are treated as a single category, then the interests of women with more resources (in this case normally white, professional women) tend to dominate the policy agenda.

These three factors—the public/private divide, the emphasis on equality, and the issue of diversity among women—resonate with major debates in feminism. The EU policy on women thus provides plenty of room for contestation, and over the years it has been very gradually modified (Pillinger 1992; Hoskyns 1992). What follows is an account of these adjustments which is largely informed by the dimensions just outlined. I have divided the history of EU policy into four periods: origins, intensification, hard times, and dissonance. These are schematic divisions intended to facilitate a greater understanding of the complexities of the policy process.

Origins

The origins of the EU women's policy lie in Article 119 of the Treaty of Rome. Adopted in 1957, this Article obliges Member States "to ensure the application of the principle of equal pay for equal work." The orthodoxy is that this Article was put in by the French government to ensure "fair competition," because women were paid higher wages in France than in the other states. Up to a point that was true, but no one ever asked *why* the French paid women better wages. The answer to that question lies in the activism of French women workers who in the 1930s were successful in persuading the labor movement to insist on equal pay at the end of the war. Textbooks still maintain that the origins of the Article were economic and had nothing to do with women's agency. The truth is more complex and, as is also the case later on, women's activism, unconnected with the EC enterprise, had effects on its development.

Article 119 was not used in any way in the early years of the European Community. When it was activated at the end of the 1960s, this was very directly and obviously the result of women's struggle. Appropriately, this struggle took place in Belgium, then the headquarters of the EC, and involved strong and complementary action by Belgian women trade unionists and feminist lawyers. The starting point came in 1966 when women at the Herstal munitions factory went on strike demanding equal pay. At Herstal, where a third of the labor force were women, all women's wages were below the lowest male wage. Moreover, the conditions in the factory were appalling. As one woman put it "we were all day in oil" (Coenen 1991, 98). At demonstrations in support of the strike, the women carried banners with the slogan "Give us Article 119." Thus a direct connection was made to the EC Treaty. As a result of that 1966 strike, the Belgian government slightly modified its labor law to allow equal pay cases to be referred to the European Court of Justice, the court of the European Community.

Two Belgian women lawyers, Eliane Vogel-Polsky and Marie-Thérèse Cuvelliez, acting entirely on their own initiative, took the opportunity to make such a reference. The case they took concerned the situation of an air stewardess, Gabrielle Defrenne. Air stewardesses at that time were forced to retire at forty with minimal benefits, because they were no longer deemed attractive enough to serve the (mainly male) passengers. Retired stewardesses found it hard to find comparable alternative employment and were often left in desperate circumstances. Three cases were brought on the situation of Defrenne, first to the Belgian courts and then to the European Court of Justice (EJC).[4] The cases were complex and took many years to resolve. The complexities of these cases will not be detailed here except to note that the first one in 1971 was lost when the judges decided they lacked the competence to deal with the matter. The second one in 1976 was successful, and the judges also ruled that Article 119 was directly applicable and could be used directly by claimants in the national courts of the Member States. In granting the equal pay principle of Article 119 the same force as the economic law creating the market, the Court provided the vital foundation upon which all later developments rested. It is significant that this advance resulted from interlocking but separate actions taken on the same issues by working-class and professional women.[5]

4. ECJ Cases: 80/70, judgment 25 May 1971; 43/75, judgment 8 April 1976; 149/77 judgment 15 June 1978.

5. All that Gabrielle Defrenne herself received from these cases was approximately £240 ($360) awarded her in the end by the Belgian courts.

Legal commentators have given no explanation for the Court's change of direction between its 1971 and 1976 rulings but have generally praised the Court for its "audacious" second ruling. They never mention that the period between 1971 and 1976 saw the growth of the second wave of feminism in almost all of the Member States of the EC. As a result, feminism was on the political agenda. Judges are impressionable people, and by 1976 they could see that the situation of women was an important political concern. They took the opportunity in 1976 to make the decision they did not make five years earlier. Rather than generating a bold move of its own, the Court was responding to political activism among women.

Intensification

The period from the mid-1970s on was one of "intensification." It was in these years that this early activism was built upon and a more solid base was developed in law for the women's policy. Thus, between 1975 and 1979 three strong directives (i.e., secondary pieces of European legislation) were adopted. The first directive covered equal pay, the second equal treatment in working conditions, and the third equal treatment in social security.[6] Still in the field of employment, they made the women's policy more detailed and more precise.

Adopting these pieces of legislation involved an intense process of negotiation, mostly carried out in intergovernmental committees within the European institutions. Some women, mainly at a professional level, were involved in these negotiations. To some extent, they were empowered by the strength of feminism outside. Nevertheless, as the negotiations moved up the hierarchy, women were gradually excluded. So, too, were some of the more radical provisions (Hoskyns 1985). The women who remained involved in the negotiations were, thus, disappointed with the outcomes. However, in retrospect, one can appreciate that these three directives are relatively strong pieces of legislation. They set obligations for governments and contained broad provisions for enforcement.

Although these directives were still confined to the employment field, they raised issues that went beyond such matters. For example,

6. Directives 75/117/EEC (equal pay); 76/207/EEC (working conditions) and 79/7/EEC (social security).

the working conditions directive very quickly raised the question of childcare, which women needed in order to enhance their employment opportunities. The social security directive raised the question of dependency because most social security systems were and are based on the notion of the man as breadwinner.

It is striking that, during this period, the trade union movement (as organized at the European level) opposed the strategy of a separate policy for women. More specifically, trade union organizers objected to women taking action as workers outside the trade union movement despite the fact that, on the whole, trade unions themselves were not addressing women's needs. As a result, women were not able to rely on trade union activity or structures to support their rights. Only much later did the European trade union movement begin to seriously support such mobilization. In the meantime, the separation and conflict between organized labor and the women's movement weakened both movements.

Hard Times

The third period, "hard times," takes us into the 1980s. This was a period of fundamental change. The context within which the women's policy had to maintain itself or expand was characterized by high levels of unemployment, government cutbacks, and deregulation. The ideological climate was very much against any continuation of equal opportunities action or legislation. This negative stance was facilitated by the fact that there were now fewer big displays of solidarity among women—the movement had gone underground. Women's activity was spreading out into new areas and diversifying, but this activity was often subtle and created a less visible public presence (Katzenstein 1987).

At the EC level, policy was becoming increasingly institutionalized because of the legal framework developed a decade earlier. To implement and develop the women's policy further, a Women's Bureau was set up in the European Commission (the Bureau was renamed the "Equal Opportunities Unit" in 1994). Women in the European Parliament also established a Committee on Women's Rights, and various networks were formed to monitor these new developments and exchange information. Most importantly, a budget line was established which financed research and other projects. This institutionalization also generated a more informal "women's European policy network" to take up a variety of interests and aggregate support.[7] This was effective up to a point but was able to neither sustain real contact with the grass-roots women's movements throughout Europe nor push to the centers of power.

No new strong legislation was adopted at the European level in the 1980s. More significant were the judgments of the European Court. These resulted from further references made (like the Defrenne cases) from the national courts on issues concerning the interpretation of Article 119 and the three Equality Directives. As a result of these judgments, the Court gave advisory rulings which set guidelines for courts across the EC. In its rulings on these references (which now number over sixty), the Court has played a distinctive but predictable role which has been well analyzed elsewhere (Fredman 1992; Prechal and Burrows 1990). To summarize briefly, the Court has been progressive on equal treatment in employment matters and has helped to establish rights for part-time and pregnant workers. But it has held the line very clearly against any move towards extending these rights into the domestic sphere or to unpaid workers. The European Court has made it clear that it does not regard such initiatives as falling within the competence of the European Union. In that sense, it has acted to define and reinforce the public/private divide.

The strategy of the European Commission (within which the Equal Opportunities Unit is located) has been to press for legislation but also to expand the women's policy into other areas through a series of Action Programs which enable it to fund projects and commission research. As a result of this work, there was a move in the early 1990s to develop policy and legislation that moved beyond the narrow confines of the labor market. The Commission began addressing issues which had for some time been raised by the different strands in the women's policy network. These policy concerns included pregnancy, sexual harassment, and childcare.[8]

The main failure of this period was the reluctance to take up the issue of diversity among women, particularly that of women from visible ethnic minorities. The European Union has never dealt with discrimination on the basis of race as it has with sex discrimination.

---

7. I have used the term "policy network" to describe this development because it is a term now widely used in political science. It is rarely applied to activities involving women.

8. Thus in the early 1990s a directive was adopted on pregnancy rights (92/85/EEC), a Commission recommendation on sexual harassment (92/131/EEC) and a Council recommendation on childcare (92/241/EEC).

The reasons for this are instructive and concern the lack of competence in the Treaty,[9] different state traditions and sensitivities on the issue, and a lack of effective campaigning. Thus, Black women experience the EU policy very differently from white women, since their situation as members of ethnic minorities is not protected at the EU level. The predominantly white women's network has so far given little priority to this issue. The result is that Black and migrant women are having to organize separately at the European level. Just as women at an earlier stage were unable to benefit by the position built up by the (male) trade unions, so Black women are currently unable to use the already existing (white) women's organizations as a springboard.[10]

Dissonance

The last section, "dissonance," concerns the present. The term is taken from Rosi Braidotti's book *Patterns of Dissonance* (1991) which examines the discipline of philosophy and its critiques. Braidotti regards philosophy as being currently in a state of crisis due to the systematic undermining (both in theory and practice) of the enlightenment values upon which it has been based. Alongside this are strong and relevant feminist critiques which suggest novel fields of inquiry and new directions. But there is no engagement between the two. "Male" philosophers will not accept feminist critiques, and feminists are unable, or unwilling, to participate in mainstream philosophy.

Similar analysis could be applied to the situation for women in the European Union. At the moment, neo-liberal deregulators are dominant, but they cannot provide solutions to the current crisis, nor halt the social and political disarray developing since the negotiation of the Treaty on European Union. The European entity cannot deal with critiques—not just those from feminists, but from environmentalists, regionalists and others. So there is a dissonance between Eurocrats and political activists. Solutions to these conflicts, or even dialogue, prove illusory.

9. There is, for example, no provision analogous to Article 119 which would prohibit race discrimination.

10. Between 1991 and 1993, I served as one of the coordinators for a report on Black and migrant women in the European Union, prepared for the European Women's Lobby. While the Lobby was courageous in commissioning the report, the production proved controversial internally.

There is also dissonance within the women's movement itself. The situation of women as a collectivity has changed and is changing. There are a few women in management or decision-making positions, and some attention is paid by those in authority to the issue of gender (Cockburn 1994). However, this leads to what Johanna Brenner (writing about the situation in the United States) has called "the selective incorporation of feminist demands" (1993). We can certainly see this in Europe. The gains that women appear to be making tend to be primarily benefiting white, middle-class, and educated women. While such gains are not unimportant, they have the effect of cutting off more privileged women from the concerns of others, especially those working at the grass-roots level. At the same time, there has been a steady deterioration for women with fewer privileges and little access to resources. The reality of this is often exemplified by the fact that many more privileged women across Europe now employ poor women (sometimes immigrants) to work for them in a domestic capacity. Thus, domestic work is being done by "other" women—and both men and the state escape responsibility.[11]

Dissonance within the women's movement raises the question of how we organize as women. We are more than 50 percent of the population in every state of the EU; we have some presence in formal politics. Can we still, should we still, be organizing as women, as a single category? What does the experience of women organizing in and around the European Union suggest about this?

My answer is that, at present, we still need to organize as women because we are still targeted as women. Other articles in this collection note, for example, the specific ways in which women are targeted for male abuse through sexual harassment, prostitution, battery, and rape. Patriarchy in the European Union is very strong; we can see it everywhere. But we can no longer assume that what one group of women does will necessarily resonate with other women, as happened in Belgium in the 1960s, and with second-wave feminism more generally. In order to improve upon the gains that have been made, we need to organize in ways which are sensitive to the different interests of women, to the huge span of those interests, and to be scrupulous about issues of democracy and who is representing whom.

11. This "new" class structure developing around domestic work and between women emerged very clearly from the field work done for *Confronting the Fortress* (European Women's Lobby 1995).

Conclusions

Estimations as to whether or not the European Union is a "good thing" for women have little value. The EU is an arena for politics and an increasingly important and permanent one. If women in Europe are to participate in politics, they need to be represented at this level. And because of the already existing policy, there is a base for action. Equally, one can and should use that foundation to show where the EU is deficient, not only in its attitude toward women, but in many other ways as well. The continuing opposition of Scandinavian women to EU entry, and to an expansion of EU competence, is extremely important in this respect.[12] As history shows, activism outside the EU, and not specifically directed at it, has been at least as important in effecting change as anything done from inside.

The EU policy has had some positive outcomes. It has, for example, encouraged links and transnational activity among women. It has also helped to enforce an equality standard in employment. But such accomplishments are not enough. We have to push our demands more strongly and work particularly for the women and the issues currently excluded.

---

12. Denmark, the only Scandinavian EEC member since 1973, shocked Europe when its voters rebuffed the Maastricht Treaty in June 1992. It then accepted the modified Edinburgh Treaty in 1993. More recently, Swedish voters supported a consultative referendum by 52 percent on 13 November 1994. Two weeks later Norwegians opposed entrance by the same percentage in their referendum. The Norwegian referendum raised a new record for voter turnout 88 percent). In all of the demonstrations of opposition to the EU, women were prominent.

▨ 2

EUROPEAN UNION SEXUAL HARASSMENT POLICY

Evelyn Collins

Action to address sexual harassment at work began in Europe in the early 1980s. This chapter traces the historical development of specific initiatives by the various European Union institutions to deal with the problem. It outlines the aims of the European Commission's Recommendation on the Protection of the Dignity of Women and Men at Work and the Code of Practice on Measures to Combat Sexual Harassment, adopted in 1991. It examines the content of this measure and concludes with an assessment of its impact on the Member States of the European Union.

A General Overview

The European Union's initiatives on sexual harassment should be considered within the general context of European Union social policy (Docksey 1987). The achievement of equal opportunities for women and men has been described as a fundamental goal of the European Union, one which it has worked for many years to achieve, through both the application of equality law and the promotion of positive action (McCrudden 1991). This goal forms an integral part of broader social policy concerns including such areas as labor law, industrial relations, social protection, and poverty. The general aim of EU policy is to improve living and working conditions. The European institutions consistently articulate the view that equality of opportunity is a vital prerequisite for the legal, economic, and social integration of the European Union. Actions in favor of equality for women appear set to remain a priority in the future plans of the European Union (European Commission 1994).

Equal opportunities law has developed into an advanced legal framework at the European Union level. Through its legal actions, the Union has clarified and progressively enlarged the application of the principle of equal treatment—a principle enshrined in Article 119 of the founding Treaty of Rome 1957, which relates to equal pay. A basic platform of rights now exists, and the legal framework is common to all Member States, taking precedence over national law. These rights and duties are conferred not only to governments but also to individuals.

There are now five Equality Directives, in addition to the right to equal pay contained in Article 119 of the Treaty of Rome. These cover such issues as equal pay, equal treatment in employment and vocational training, and equal treatment in statutory social security schemes.[1] In 1992 the Council of Ministers also adopted a directive on the protection of pregnant women and those who have recently given birth.[2]

The platform of rights accessible under European equality law has had a major impact in many of the Member States. The laws have influenced such issues as equal pay, rights of part-time workers, indirect discrimination and pregnancy discrimination, as well as the availability and extent of remedies that are available to women (Banks 1991; Collins 1991).

In addition to its legislative work and ensuring the adequate implementation of equality laws, the European Commission has developed a series of action programs on equal opportunities for women. These programs are intended to strengthen individual

1. See the five following Directives: (1) Council Directive of 10 February 1975 (75/117/EEC) on the approximation of the laws of the Member States relating to the principle of equal pay for men and women (OJ L 45/19, 19 February 1975); (2) Council Directive of 9 February 1976 (76/207/EEC) on the implementation of the principle of equal treatment for men and women as regards access to employment, vocational training and promotion, and working conditions (OJ L 39/40, 14 February 1976); (3) Council Directive of 19 December 1978 (79/7/EEC) on the progressive implementation of the principle of equal treatment for men and women in matters of social security (OJ L 6/24, 10 January 1979); (4) Council Directive of 24 July 1986 (86/378/EEC) on the implementation of the principle of equal treatment in occupational social security schemes (OJ L 225/40, 12 August 1986); (5) Council Directive of 11 December 1986 on the application of the principle of equal treatment between men and women engaged in an activity including agriculture, in a self-employed capacity, and on the protection of self-employed women during pregnancy and motherhood (OJ L 359, 19 December 1986).

2. Council Directive of 19 October 1992 (92/85/EEC) on the protection at work of pregnant women or women who have recently given birth (OJ L 348/1, 28 November 1992). This measure was adopted primarily as a health and safety measure.

rights through the development of legal action and, in addition, to promote equal opportunities through practical initiatives designed to overcome the structural inequalities between women and men in society.[3] Currently, a Third Action Programme on Equal Opportunities is nearing completion and a Fourth is under consideration (European Commission 1994). The explicit aims of the Third Action Programme are to promote women's full participation in economic and social life and to give proper recognition to the value of their contribution to the labor market.

Yet, as others point out, the European Union's policies on women are vulnerable to attack on a number of feminist grounds (Hoskyns 1992).[4] The policies are primarily focused on (un)employment issues and do not deal with other matters affecting women's lives such as male violence; they are based primarily on notions of formal equality (e.g., comparison of like-with-like) and do not often enough take women's specific circumstances into account. In their generality, EU policies also lack reference to "socially excluded" groups such as ethnic minority women.

Nevertheless, it is in this overall context that the Union's initiatives on sexual harassment should be considered. More specifically, the European Commission's Recommendation on the Protection of the Dignity of Women and Men at Work and the Code of Practice on Measures to Combat Sexual Harassment represented a particular culmination of feminist activism through the 1980s.

An Historical Overview of Sexual Harassment in the EU

In 1980, few people in Europe discussed sexual harassment as a problem; it did not have a name, and those subjected to it had no legal protection. By contrast, in the United States, discussion on the nature of the problem and ways to deal with it had begun in the 1970s. By the decade's close, activists on both sides of the Atlantic were aware that the Equal Employment Opportunities Commission had developed guidelines and a legal position on what constituted sexual harassment.

3. New Community Action Programme on the Promotion of Equal Opportunities for Women, 1982–1985, Supplement 1/81—Bulletin EC; Medium Term Action Programme on Equal Opportunities for Women, 1986–1990, Supplement 3/86—Bulletin EC; and Third Medium Term Action Programme on Equal Opportunities for Women, 1990–95, COM (90) 449 final, 6 November 1990.
4. See also the numerous essays contained in this volume.

In the early 1980s, a number of Member States began to focus on the problem and pursue particular initiatives. In August 1983, the Trade Union Congress in the United Kingdom published a guide on sexual harassment amidst many frivolous comments in the press. These included remarks such as "trade unions say hands off brothers." Significantly, BBC Northern Ireland asked the Equal Opportunities Commission for Northern Ireland for an interview on sexual harassment at this time. The Commission contended that sexual harassment amounted to unlawful sex discrimination. As a result of that interview, the first complainant came forward, a young woman apprentice motor mechanic in a Belfast garage. She had been subjected to lewd comments and unwanted physical contact from two male colleagues which resulted in injury. She succeeded in her complaint of sexual harassment. The Industrial Tribunal found both that the men's behavior was entirely unacceptable and that the harassment was dictated by prejudice because she was female. The Tribunal concluded that sexual harassment constituted unlawful discrimination (*M v. Crescent Garage Ltd* IT Case 23/83/SD). This was the first case of sexual harassment in the United Kingdom to be brought under sex discrimination legislation.

At the European Union level, pressure mounted for a Union-wide response to the problem. In 1984, for example, the Council passed a resolution on positive action for women generally, calling on Member States to take steps to ensure respect for the dignity of women in the workplace. At an informal meeting of the Council of Ministers on Women's Issues at the Hague, in March 1986, under the Dutch Presidency of the Council, the issue of sexual harassment was discussed, and the Council asked the European Commission to conduct an investigation on the subject. The Commission duly contracted EU expert Michael Rubenstein to undertake this project. His study made a significant contribution to the understanding of the nature and the scale of the problem within the EC labor market (Rubenstein 1988).

In addition to the European Commission's work, there have also been several discussions, resolutions, and calls for action by the European Parliament and from its Women's Rights Committee in particular. In 1986, for example, it adopted a resolution on violence against women that called for an assessment of the protections available to counter sexual harassment under national labor and anti-discrimination law (OJ C 176/79, 14 July 1986). Indeed, the European Parliament has played a critical role in encouraging the other institutions, including the European Commission, into action. By the late 1980s, some members of Parliament were explicitly requesting a directive on sexual harassment (Written Question 2119/90; OJ C 90/37, 8 April 1991). Indeed, this demand was one of the main recommendations made by Michael Rubenstein in his report on sexual harassment in the European Community (1988).

Research had revealed that there was an absence of appropriate remedies or legal sanctions against sexual harassment in most Member States and that few meaningful voluntary initiatives had been taken (Rubenstein 1988). Rubenstein's report concluded that there was a need for a directive to provide adequate protection for those who suffer sexual harassment. The Commission, in response, found no need for a separate directive. It considered that sexual harassment constituted unlawful sex discrimination and was therefore already covered by the Equal Treatment Directive of 1976 (76/207/EEC). It should be acknowledged, in addition, that the European Commission was experiencing difficulties with a number of its proposals for new directives on equal treatment issues around this time (*CREW Reports* 1987, 5–7; *CREW Reports* 1988, 5–6). While the Commission's role is to propose and draft new laws, it is up to the Council to adopt them. A number of Member States were involved in moving their own countries toward greater deregulation of the labor market. They were, therefore, reluctant to adopt new laws in the social policy area.

Community-wide Measures

It was the Irish Government which encouraged the European Commission to take the final steps towards producing a Union-wide initiative on sexual harassment. When it held the Presidency of the Council in the first half of 1990, the Irish Government put forward a resolution on the subject. It called on the Commission to produce a Code of Practice based on examples of good practice on means of dealing with the problem across the Community. This resolution was adopted on 29 May 1990 (OJ C 157/3, 27 June 1990). In general, the Member States warmly welcomed the Presidency's initiative, the significance of which was more symbolic than legal. It was clear, indeed, that there was an increasing level of awareness of the problem by the end of the 1980s. It is thus possible that the proposed action in this area appeared attractive to governments and employers/trade unions who wished to be seen as taking the issue seriously, especially as the costs associated with implementing this measure were likely to be minimal.

It is clear, however, that despite the growing recognition of sexual harassment as a problem, it remains a serious issue for working women across the European Union. Studies have been undertaken in almost every Member State about the nature and incidence of sexual harassment; clearly, it is not an isolated phenomenon but rather an unpleasant and unavoidable aspect of the working lives of millions of women in the Union (see Rubenstein 1988; Rubenstein 1992a). The consequences of harassment both for those subjected to it and, indeed, for employers, are well documented and do not need to be repeated here. In general terms, however, it is evident that sexual harassment is an obstacle to the proper integration of women into the labor market. The European Commission has expressly committed itself to encouraging the development of comprehensive measures to improve such integration.[5]

The European Commission was also under increased pressure from feminist groups outside of it to confront sexual harassment, for example, from the AVFT in France, WASH in the United Kingdom and Handen Thus in the Netherlands. It became increasingly difficult for the European Commission not to take action. The water had been tested with the Council Resolution of 1990, and the time appeared right to produce an additional Union-wide response to the problem.[6]

It was felt that the adoption of a European Commission recommendation would help to ensure that the problem of sexual harassment was dealt with as a sex discrimination issue, as a significant obstacle to women's participation in the labor market—a barrier which equal treatment laws were devised to overcome. While traditionally only Community regulations and directives are legally binding, an interesting legal point arose at the time of drafting of the Recommendation.[7]

The argument that national courts and tribunals should be expected to render judgments which coincide with recommendations was gaining momentum. In 1990, the European Court of Justice concretized this position in *Grimaldi v. Fonds de Maladies*

5. This is one of the main objectives of the Third Action Programme on Equal Opportunities, mentioned above.

6. For a description of the growth in support of action on sexual harassment, see Rubenstein (1992b).

7. Previously, according to Article 189 of the EEC Treaty, a recommendation had no binding legal force.

Professionnelles (Case 322/88 [1990] IRLR 400). In that case, which concerned a Commission health and safety recommendation, the Court ruled that the Commission's recommendations, while not of binding nature such as a directive, cannot be considered as lacking in legal effect. The Court held that national courts are bound to take recommendations into consideration in order to decide disputes submitted to them, in particular where such recommendations clarify the interpretation of national provisions designed to implement and/or supplement binding Community measures. Since a Code of Practice is annexed to the Recommendation, and since it supplements the binding Equal Treatment Directive of 1976, it follows that national courts should take the contents of the EC Recommendation and Code of Practice into account where relevant.

One of the principal aims of the Recommendation is to encourage the promotion of awareness that sexual harassment is contrary to the principle of equal treatment in the Equal Treatment Directive of 1976. The European Commission endeavored to raise awareness that, under certain circumstances, the problem may be dealt with under national equality laws. Clearly, sexual harassment is discrimination based on sex because the gender of the recipient is the determining factor in who is harassed. In some countries, such as the United Kingdom, it was treated as such; but, in other countries, the use of equal treatment laws remained an untested hypothesis.

The second important aim of the Recommendation and Code of Practice is to provide the basis for a definition which may be used in the Member States to determine what conduct constitutes sexual harassment in the workplace. The European Commission followed the terms of the 1990 Council Resolution on this issue. Sexual harassment is defined as unwanted conduct of a sexual nature or other conduct based on sex affecting the dignity of women and men at work. Thus, a range of behavior may constitute sexual harassment, including unwanted physical, verbal, or non-verbal conduct. The central characteristic is that it is unwanted by the recipient— each individual thus determines what behavior they regard as either acceptable or offensive to them.

The Recommendation clearly sets out that sexual harassment is unacceptable if the conduct is unwanted, unreasonable, and offensive to the recipient. The law covers both harassment perpetrated by employers as well as employees. Sexual harassment is prohibited when it is used either explicitly or implicitly as a basis for a decision which affects that person's access to employment or to vocational training, continued employment, promotion, salary, or any other employment decisions, and/or where such conduct creates an intimidating, hostile, or humiliating working environment for the recipient (Article 1). Thus, both *quid pro quo* harassment and hostile working environment harassment are covered.

It was the Commission's view that, although neither the Recommendation nor the Code of Practice provided an exhaustive list of behaviors which may constitute sexual harassment, the general definition would prove a useful guide for employers, employees, and trade unions as well as lawyers and judges in national legal systems, to determine whether particular conduct is or is not sexual harassment.

This general definition, with its reliance on assessing the impact of sexual harassment as perceived by the recipient rather than by a more objective standard, such as a list of outlawed behaviors, has been the subject of some criticism (Lester 1993). All serious commentators appear to agree that it is the impact of the harasser's conduct rather than the intent which is crucial in determining sexual harassment. Differences arise, however, with identifying the standard to be applied to determine if certain conduct is unreasonable or offensive. The Recommendation and Code of Practice set out to encourage courts to consider the propriety of the conduct at issue from the recipient's perspective. Some commentators, however, have argued that parts of the text seem to conflict with this. For example, the Code states that "sexual attention becomes sexual harassment if it is persisted once it has been made clear that it is regarded by the recipient as offensive, although one incident of harassment may constitute sexual harassment if sufficiently serious" (OJ L 49/4, 24 February 1992). It is argued that this wording appears to put the onus on the recipient to complain about the behavior before it could be considered to be sexual harassment. In addition, the Code ignores the variety of reasons why those who are harassed are often extremely reluctant to complain. It remains to be seen how this issue will be dealt with by the national courts. It certainly underlines the importance of preventative policies to deal with the problem and of (informal) mechanisms that will give individuals the confidence to complain without fear of retaliation.

Another means of overcoming this potential problem is to specifically outlaw certain behaviors per se. These could be determined through research on the types of conduct women generally find offensive. This approach would make it clear that the absence of a complaint does not indicate acceptance of particular conduct. Instead, sexual conduct is offensive per se unless a woman expressly states that she welcomes it (*New York Times*, 8 May 1994, E3).

Initially, the draft Code of Practice sent out for consultation by the European Commission contained a list of behaviors which was intended to be illustrative of the types of conduct women find offensive. This did not survive the consultation process, a matter of much regret to many commentators. There is no clear explanation for its removal, although as might have been anticipated, there were problems concerning its detail. In any event, a list has now been reproduced in a further publication by the European Commission, *How to Combat Sexual Harassment at Work: A Guide to Implementing the EC Code* (1993). This manual also provides specific examples of actions and policies from all Member States.

The final aim of the Recommendation is to encourage the Member States to implement the Code of Practice in the public sector, which should serve as an example to the private sector. The Code contains a series of practical guidelines on how to deal with the problem. The main thrust of the initiative is that it is in the interests of everyone to take proactive steps to deal with sexual harassment in the workplace.

The Code of Practice annexed to the Recommendation contains practical guidance on initiating and pursuing positive measures designed to create a climate at work in which sexual harassment does not occur. It was based on successful measures taken across the Member States and makes a series of recommendations to employers, trade unions, and employees on practical steps which can be taken in the workplace to prevent the problem from arising and to ensure that it is adequately dealt with if it does. The Code was finalized following extensive consultations with employer and trade union representatives, national governments, national equality agencies, the European Parliament, and the Economic and Social Committee.

The Code addresses a number of important issues. It links sexual harassment to power and position in the hierarchy. It specifically lists a range of vulnerable groups—mentioning new entrants to the labor market, young women, divorced women, women from racial minorities, and women with disabilities. Timely lobbying during the consultation process by members of the European Parliament and the International Lesbian and Gay Association also strengthened the arguments in favor of dealing with the harassment of lesbians and gay men.

As regards content, preventative measures include recommendations on introducing a policy statement, on communicating it across the organization, on designating special responsibility for combating sexual harassment, and on organizing effective training to deal with the issues. On procedural steps, the Code recommends that means be made available for the informal resolution of problems, for advice and assistance to complainants, for formal complaint procedures, investigations, and disciplinary action. There are also recommendations aimed at trade unions and at employees themselves.

In many European countries, counseling and advisory facilities are becoming the cornerstone of sexual harassment policies. In the Netherlands, for example, virtually all of the largest private and public employers have established a network of confidential counselors. They are given special training and normally deal with sexual harassment issues, typically on a part-time basis in addition to their other duties (de Vires 1993).[8]

An Assessment

It is clear from events subsequent to the adoption of the Recommendation and Code of Practice that there is heightened awareness of, and activity around, the problem in the Member States. The European Commission's initiative has had symbolic importance and would appear set to have some legal and practical impact as well. Discussions have taken place across the Member States on ways of implementing the Recommendation.

In Denmark, the first cases of sexual harassment as sex discrimination have been argued before the courts; in France, amendments to both the Penal Code and the Labor Code have been made. In the United Kingdom, the Department of Employment has issued guidance on sexual harassment drawing on the Recommendation and Code of Practice; in Ireland, the Department of Equality and Law Reform has now issued its Code of Practice on the issue of sexual harassment, with the support of both employer and trade union organizations; in 1992, in Belgium, a Royal Decree required all employers to state in their work rules "the measures laid down to protect employees against sexual harassment at work"; in Spain, a legal duty has been placed on the employer "to ensure respect for a person's privacy and dignity including protection against verbal or physical insults of a sexual nature"; and, in the Netherlands, an obligation to protect employees against the risk of sexual harassment

---

8. These counselors are neither attorneys nor therapists. Rather, they are people trained to provide advice, assistance, and support to complainants.

is to be embodied in health and safety laws (*European Industrial Relations Review* 1992; *Labour Research* 1992). We can expect that the European Commission itself will be monitoring developments in the Member States. Indeed, it will soon report on the effectiveness of the Recommendation and Code of Practice. It is clear from the terms of the Recommendation that the Commission will be looking at the degree of awareness of the Code, its perceived effectiveness, its degree of application, and the extent of its use in collective bargaining between the social partners.

It is also evident, from a recent report of the Women's Rights Committee of the European Parliament (1994), that lobbying of the European Commission will continue in order to produce further regulations in this area. The report calls on Member States to introduce national laws obliging employers to include in their internal rules preventative measures and penalties against those found guilty of sexual harassment. In addition, the report suggests the appointment of counselors to deal with complaints. For small companies unable to appoint such counselors, the local labor inspector should assume the role. Member States were also urged to provide information on the possibilities of redress available to victims of sexual harassment in the workplace, through labor councils, or through courts. The Parliament called on both the European institutions themselves and national governments to set an example to private enterprise by being the first to appoint workplace counselors (Women's Rights Committee 1994). It remains to be seen whether this challenge is taken up by the European Union institutions and by national governments.

Indeed, much remains to be done to eliminate sexual harassment and to provide adequate protection to victims. However, in my view, the European Union's initiatives represent steps in the right direction.

3

THE INTERPLAY
The Formation of Sexual Harassment Legislation in France and EU Policy Initiatives[1]

Amy G. Mazur

This chapter explores the ways in which the policy initiatives of the European Union affected the formation of French sexual harassment legislation adopted in 1992.[2] To this end, it traces how sexual harassment in the workplace was first defined as a public problem in the mid-1980s in France and examines the ways in which the issue was then placed on and immediately removed from the government agenda in 1985, restored to the government agenda in 1989, and legislated and implemented in 1992.[3] The analysis argues that the low government priority given to sexual harassment led to the merely symbolic content of the legislation currently in force. The story of sexual harassment legislation in France demonstrates that the development of French policy coincided with the

1. I would like to thank Indiana University-Purdue University at Indianapolis, the Center for West European Studies at Indiana University, Bloomington, and the American Political Science Association for grants which allowed me to make two research visits to Paris in the summers of 1993 and 1994 to conduct the research for this chapter.

2. Interviews for this chapter were conducted with policy actors involved with the formation of sexual harassment policy including representatives of feminist organizations, policymakers in the women's rights and labor ministries, trade union representatives, policy experts, political party activists, and work inspectors. A list of these interviews, conducted in 1988–1989 and the summers of 1993 and 1994, is available from the author upon request.

3. In1992, the French parliament adopted two different pieces of legislation addressing sexual harassment at work. The first was an amendment on sexual harassment introduced into the penal code by Socialist deputy, Yvette Roudy. The amendment then became an article in its final draft. The second was a separate law which regulated sexual harassment in the workplace and was proposed by the Deputy Minister of Women's Rights Véronique Neiertz. Prior to these two laws, there had been no formal recognition that sexual harassment at work is discrimination.

formation of EU policy on sexual harassment. Indeed, at certain critical moments, EU initiatives played an important role in the policy process.

EU initiatives to combat sexual harassment in the workplace in the mid-1980s, ranging from subsidies for groups and conferences on sexual harassment in Member States to formal policy statements and reports, led to the European Commission Recommendation on the Protection of the Dignity of Women and Men at Work in 1991 and the attached Code of Practice.[4] The Commission Recommendation defines sexual harassment as "unacceptable behavior" and, through the Code of Practice, specifies the actions that employers and trade unions should take to reduce the incidence of sexual harassment in the workplace (Carter 1992; Parlement Européen 1994: 117–124). Within France, these initiatives contributed to the identification of sexual harassment as a salient public problem worthy of legislative redress. However, supranational policy efforts had a limited effect on the formulation and implementation of the new French legislation on sexual harassment. Despite EU pressure for a broad definition of sexual harassment and a wide range of suggested national measures, French legislation in both content and application has been circumscribed. For example, both the penal code article and the specific law adopted in 1992 were limited to direct or *quid pro quo* harassment of employees by their superiors. Consequently, these laws ignored direct harassment by colleagues and indirect harassment caused by a hostile work environment.[5]

This article traces the formation of current sexual harassment policy through three distinctive policy stages—pre-formulation, formulation, and post-formulation—to assess the role of EU policy

4. Unlike regulations which are "immediately binding on member states" or directives which set legal principles which must be contained in the legislation of Member States, recommendations in the past have had "no binding force" (Carter 1992, 440). However, as Collins points out in this book, the 1991 EU Recommendation and Code of Practice may be gaining as much legal authority as a directive.

5. Catharine A. MacKinnon (1979) first developed this two-pronged definition of "quid pro quo" sexual harassment and "hostile environment" harassment which has been subsequently enforced in the United States. In the first type of harassment, courts can punish individuals who directly threaten colleagues and employees with material retribution if they do not perform sexually. In the second type of harassment, individuals (usually the employer) are susceptible to penalty if they permit a work environment in which employees feel sexually intimidated through, for example, the public display of pornographic material.

and initiatives in French policymaking.[6] It then concludes with an appraisal of the EU's impact on each policy stage and considers the broader implications concerning the extent to which the EU can promote concrete policies that effectively reduce gender-based employment discrimination in EU member countries.

Pre-Formulation: Problem Definition

Sexual harassment was not defined as a public problem in France until 1985. In the United States, for example, feminist conscious-ness-raising groups in the 1970s had named sexual harassment as a serious impediment to women's freedom and equality. In France, the new feminist movements of the 1970s did not specifically dis-cuss sexual harassment in the workplace. In general, *the mouvement de libération des femmes* (MLF), the French women's liberation movement, did not focus on workplace discrimination against women or policy solutions that would address gender-based em-ployment inequities. Certain segments of the MLF, however, did deal with sexual violence against women, primarily, in the private sphere. The identification of sexual harassment at work as a prob-lem did not occur until after the activities of the MLF dissipated in the beginning of the 1980s.[7]

Until 1985, a critical mass of the French population still did not recognize sexual harassment in the workplace as a social condition. Much of the French political elite were not attuned to the issue as an unacceptable problem. For instance, in 1985, Jacques Séguela, the manager of President François Mitterrand's electoral campaign, made the following public statement about sexual harassment at work:

6. "Pre-formulation" begins with problem definition. In a democracy, social con-ditions are defined as public problems before becoming the objects of government action. Once a public problem is identified, solutions to those problems get placed onto the government agenda. Once on the agenda, the next stage of the policy process begins. In "formulation," policy actors in state and society produce formal policy statements like laws and executive orders. Once a statement is issued, the policy enters the third stage of the process, "post-formulation." This includes implementa-tion and evaluation. A policy can be implemented, enforced, and used as a guide for interpretation in court decisions. Also, actors concerned about the impact of that pol-icy evaluate and eventually rework it to better address the particular public problem. The policy formation process, then, can potentially begin anew in this third stage.

7. For analyses of the French feminist movements, see Duchen (1986) and Jenson (1989). For a specific discussion of the position of the MLF on women's equal employment issues, see Mazur (1996).

Of course, I have had occasion to hump cute chicks on my office car-
pet. Sexual harassment is the demeanor of all Latin men towards
women. In my country, we call that courtship. It is French men's
need to seduce at work as well as in the subway. But be careful, in the
final analysis, it is the woman who decides (in Zelensky and Gaussot
1986, 138).[8]

The turning point in the French public's recognition of sexual
harassment as a problem came in 1985. There were four specific
events which contributed to this important recognition.

First, early in 1985 several feminists from within academia and
the European Parliament created the *Association Européenne contre
les Violences Faites aux Femmes au Travail* (AVFT). A self-consciously
feminist pressure group that organizes specifically around sexual
harassment issues, the AVFT has lobbied for an authoritative government stance on sexual harassment. The AVFT has served as a
consultant for management, labor administrators, and women's
rights administrators interested in developing prevention programs.
The group has sponsored numerous public information campaigns
and has established a hot-line to help victims of harassment with
counseling, legal advice, and support. By 1990 the AVFT had published a proposal for sexual harassment legislation.

According to founding members, the AVFT looked to Europe
because of the impressive network at the EU level (e.g., the
Women's Rights Commission in the European Parliament and the
Equal Opportunities Unit in the European Commission).[9] More
importantly, from the group's inception, founders emphasized the
European dimension to obtain crucial start-up funding from the
European Commission. To date, EU subsidies have provided a large
portion of the AVFT's budget in a country where fund-raising is rare
and state subsidies are limited.

A second event which contributed to the public recognition of
sexual harassment as a problem was the 1985 First National Colloquium on Sexual Harassment held in Paris.[10] Organized principally
by the *Ligue du Droit des Femmes* (LDF), one of the few reform-ori-
ented feminist groups created in the 1970s, the conference played

8. All translations are by the author.

9. Interviews with co-presidents Marie-Victoire Louis (May 1989, July 1993,
and July 1994) and Sylvie Cromer (July 1994).

10. For a report of the conference, see Zelensky and Gaussot (1986). Also in 1985,
the Club Flora Tristan, a collective of feminist researchers, held their own mini-con-
ference on sexual harassment in the workplace, "Sexual harassment, just another
ordinary experience."

a pivotal role in sensitizing the public to this issue. It documented extensively the incidence of sexual harassment at work, criticized the absence of adequate legal instruments to fight such discrimination, and proposed concrete solutions, including the advancement of specific legislation. The LDF also conducted the first public opinion survey on sexual harassment in conjunction with the women's weekly magazine, BIBA.

National newspapers estimated that two hundred people attended the conference, including members of certain trade unions, the Socialist government, left-wing political parties, and feminist groups (Zelensky and Gaussot 1986, 10–11). Many actively participated in formal presentations. The conference received extensive and unprecedented coverage in the print and electronic media. Yvette Fuillet, jurist, co-founder of the AVFT, member of the European Parliament, and active supporter of sexual harassment policy at the EU level, was one of the keynote speakers. The Colloquium received funding from the Ministry of Women's Rights and the European Commission.

The presence of Socialist Minister of Women's Rights (MWR) Yvette Roudy at the conference marked the third important political development in that year. Starting in 1985, Roudy began to focus the attention of her ministry on sexual violence against women. Previously, she had exhausted her own agenda for feminist policy with the adoption of the 1983 Equal Employment Law and a sex discrimination bill in 1985. At the time of the colloquium, Roudy was searching for a new area of feminist policy.[11] The colloquium, then, provided a venue for her new policy focus. Not only did she subsidize the conference and appear as a keynote speaker, she also concluded the conference by announcing her intention to develop sexual harassment legislation that would address the lacunae in current policy.

The fourth development in 1985 was the increased attention in the European Community to sexual harassment in the workplace. A 1984 European Commission report on women in paid labor showed that one in ten women surveyed in Member States had been sexually harassed on the job (in Zelensky and Gaussot 1986, 10–11). Yvette Fuillet quoted this report in the opening of the LDF Colloquium. The Council, also in 1984, issued a Recommendation on the

11. "Feminist policy" refers to any state-sponsored action which aims to explicitly improve women's rights and status however they might be defined. For example, feminist policies include, but are not limited to, maternity leave, reproductive rights, equal employment policy, and policies which deal with sexual harassment at work.

Promotion of Positive Action for Women which mentioned specifically the problem of sexual harassment (in Carter 1992, 441).
Although information and recommendations were formally disseminated to Member States in 1984, EU policy statements did not
begin to resonate in France until 1985 when the Commission funded
the LDF conference and subsidized the AVFT. Efforts to counter
sexual harassment in France are clearly linked to larger EU actions
to bring the issue to the public's attention in Member States.

The Government's Agenda[12]

With the problem of sexual harassment defined in 1985 and promises
of draft legislation being made by the Women's Rights Minister, on-
the-job sexual harassment had been placed on the government's
agenda for the first time in France. This activity did not lead, however, to the formulation of government policy. It took another seven
years for the government to even agree to draft legislation. It did so
in April 1992. Kingdon (1984) argues that in order for a policy
proposal to move from the government agenda to a decision agenda
(i.e., the actual list of policy items that the government plans to act
on), there has to be an open window through which key policy
actors or "policy entrepreneurs" push their policy ideas from the
first stage to the second. Policy windows can be opened by social
problems or by political events. In the case of sexual harassment
legislation in France, the political conditions were not present to
open such a window until 1991.

  Why did the policy window for sexual harassment legislation
remain closed for so many years? First, sexual harassment did not
emerge as an important campaign issue in the run-up to the 1986
legislative elections. Second, from 1986 to 1991 top officials in
charge of the women's policy portfolio were hostile or, at best, apathetic to calls for government action on sexual harassment. Considering the key role these ministries have played in setting the
government's agenda for women's rights policy since 1974, ministerial resistance contributed greatly to keeping the policy window
closed for sexual harassment. From 1986 to 1988, under a right-
wing government and a left-wing President, the Women's Rights
Ministry was downgraded to a Delegation in the Social Affairs
Ministry. The new Delegate, Hélène Gisserot, studiously avoided

12. This refers to the list of items the government is considering.

discussing the problem of sexual harassment. Support for reform was thus impossible. After the Socialists won back a partial parliamentary majority in 1988 and the Delegation was restored to a cabinet-level position, one rank lower than a ministry, the new Deputy Minister of Women's Rights (DMWR), Michèle André, also resisted pressure for attention to the sexual harassment issue. For instance, in a public interview in 1989 André denied that sexual harassment was an important issue for her office and questioned the utility of specific legislation (*Le Nouvel Observateur*, 2–8 March 1989).

In addition, in the late 1980s, few powerful interests, like pressure groups, trade unions, and political parties, articulated demands for sexual harassment policy. A small coalition of feminist groups, led by the AVFT and joined by one of the five labor confederations, the *Confédération Française Démocratique du Travail* (CFDT), constituted the most vocal support for government action in this area. By this time, the LDF had become virtually inactive.

While advocates at the European level continued to push for redress in the late 1980s, without a concrete legal instrument, like a Commission recommendation and code of practice, directives or regulations, reformers possessed no formal authority over Member State policy. It was not until 1991 that the EU issued an authoritative policy statement on sexual harassment, the November 27th Commission Recommendation on the Protection of the Dignity of Women and Men at Work and attached Code of Practice. Before this, its many initiatives remained largely symbolic. These included the 1986 European Parliament Resolution, the 1987 Commission report on sexual harassment, the 1988 Consultative Council's recommendation and the Council's 1990 Resolution for a recommendation. All of these actions held no formal sway over Member State policy. Nonetheless, these same symbolic measures compelled the recalcitrant Deputy Minister of Women's Rights to place sexual harassment legislation on her government agenda. Still, without a directive, EU policy could not oblige the Socialists to present a bill.

Indeed, the International Colloquium on Sexual Harassment, organized by the AVFT in March 1989, may have provided a more direct influence on André's decision to support sexual harassment reform. With significant European Commission funding and a strong presence from the Commission's Equal Opportunities Unit, the Deputy Minister made an eleventh-hour decision to provide a small subsidy for the conference. She also made a brief appearance. Organizers of the conference asserted that André lent her support because of the international attention French responses to sexual harassment had received from the conference.[13] Organizers brought in speakers from Europe and the United States.[14] Members of the AVFT asserted that one of the major objectives of the conference was to force the government to take action.

At the conference, André was almost obligated to promise a government bill on sexual harassment. In the two years that followed, however, she failed to present one. Instead, André made a series of gestures to honor her 1989 promise. For example, she called a working group of the CSEP (High Council for Equal Employment) two weeks after the conference. The working group, composed of representatives from labor, management, the government, feminist associations, and pertinent experts on sexual harassment, did not meet again until April 1991.

In 1990, feminist-oriented upper civil servants in the Women's Rights Ministry, or femocrats, produced draft legislation on sexual harassment to be inserted into the penal and labor codes. However, because André refused to present these proposals, they were forgotten. According to one femocrat, if André had wanted to support the sexual harassment bills, the government would have placed them on its parliamentary agenda (Interview, Laret-Bedel, July 1993).[15]

Throughout André's tenure, the femocrats in the women's ministry unsuccessfully used EU policy statements and reports on sexual harassment to buttress their arguments to the Women's Minister. They invited EU expert Michael Rubenstein to an official meeting of the CSEP working group on sexual harassment in the spring of 1991. In a recent interview, Rubenstein said that with the exception of those in the women's ministry who had invited him, the participants at the meeting felt that EU policy was overly restrictive (July 1993). Their primary objection was that the EU defines sexual harassment broadly, in terms of hostile environment as well as *quid pro quo.*

13. See interview with AVFT co-president Marie-Victoire Louis (May 1989 and July 1993).

14. They included, for example, Catharine A. MacKinnon from the United States, Christopher Docksey from the European Commission, Gabrielle Elstner from Germany, Alie Kupier from the Netherlands, and May Orbine from Ireland. I also attended this two-day conference. For a written report of the conference, see AVFT (1990).

15. Catherine Laret-Bedel is a jurist and staff member of the equal employment council, the CSEP (High Council for Equal Employment).

Decision Agenda Status

There were three political events in 1991 and one in 1992 that opened a definitive policy window for sexual harassment legislation in France. Perhaps the most important of these occurred at the European Community level with the Commission formally issuing its Recommendation in November 1991.[16] Although the actual authority of the Recommendation for Member State policy was indirect, the attention to EU directives intensified with the December Summit at Maastricht. At this 1991 summit, the Commission focused on expanding the political integration of the Community and further developing Community social policy.

Second, with the nomination of the new Prime Minister, Edith Cresson, in May 1991, a new Deputy Minister of Women's Rights was appointed, Véronique Neiertz. As Deputy Minister, Neiertz was the driving force behind the adoption of the 1992 sexual harassment law. The law was nicknamed, as a result, the "*loi Neiertz.*" In an interview in July 1993, Neiertz stated that in her first weeks as minister, she discovered that trade union representatives and employers, in addition to the AVFT, identified the need for law in this area. She saw herself as a policy entrepreneur who negotiated a solution between "extremist" (*sic*) feminists demanding an authoritative law and those who were opposed to any legislation at all. Feminists called for a law that covered both quid pro quo and hostile environment harassment. Further, they demanded strict penalties for violation.

In 1991, Neiertz formally funded a Harris poll on the incidence of sexual harassment (Louis-Harris 1991), the first official and scientific poll conducted in France on this issue. She also had her office resurrect their bill proposals from 1990. For staff members who worked on the 1992 bill, Neiertz's support, particularly in comparison to her predecessor's apathy, was pivotal in the placement of the new labor code bill on the parliamentary agenda in January 1992 (Interview, Laret-Bedel, July 1993).

Third, in the summer of 1992, the Socialist parliamentary group in the National Assembly, led by Yvette Roudy and with the approval of Jean-Michel Belorgey, chair of the Social Affairs Commission, proposed an amendment into an ongoing penal code reform then debated in the National Assembly. A product of wider EU pressures, this bill increased pressure for Neiertz to produce her

---

16. The Recommendation and the attached Code of Practice did not, however, take effect until they were published in the EU parliamentary records of 2 February 1992.

own bill. Additionally, the Anita Hill/Clarence Thomas trials in the fall of 1992 propelled sexual harassment into the French public's consciousness, but in a very critical light. According to one member of the AVFT, linking discussion of French sexual harassment policy to United States policy would undermine public support for legislation (Interview, Marie-Victoire Louis, July 1993). The French feared adoption of a U.S.-based policy which they regarded as excessively restrictive.

Thus, in 1992, the Socialist government agreed to sponsor sexual harassment legislation drafted by Véronique Neiertz's office, which proposed inserting a legal definition of sexual harassment at work into French law. Nonetheless, the political circumstances that preceded the Neiertz bill gave it a relatively low status in the Socialists' parliamentary queue.

Formulation

Feminist demands for legislation were excluded consistently from the formulation process because their position did not correspond to the political consensus. The AVFT's lack of political influence made it nearly impossible for sexual harassment advocates to convince mainstream policymakers in the Deputy Ministry of Women's Rights (DMWR), the Socialist government, and the Parliament to accept feminist recommendations for new policy. Furthermore, without any widespread public support for sexual harassment reform, nonfeminist interest groups, political parties, and state actors were not compelled to act. Consequently, as Véronique Neiertz and members of parliament openly admitted, the new legislation was a modest attempt to deal with sexual harassment. Throughout the formulation process, it was clear that state actors sought to produce symbolic policy statements and not authoritative policy designed to reduce the incidence of sexual harassment.

Both the 1992 legislation proposed by Neiertz and the article on sexual harassment in the 1992 penal code reform initiated by Roudy, defined sexual harassment uniquely in terms of *quid pro quo* harassment. Thus, any future treatment of hostile environment harassment by French law was essentially eliminated. In her opening remarks in the Senate debate on the sexual harassment bill, Deputy Minister Neiertz expressed the commonly held hostility towards the two-pronged approach to sexual harassment by referring to it as "*un puritanisme anglo-saxon.*" Similar concerns were expressed by other members of parliament. Policymakers, therefore, perceived the regulation of sexual harassment as a potential threat to personal freedoms and French culture.

When asked about the impending reform by senators, employers also voiced their opposition to the broader definition of sexual harassment, arguing that such intervention in the workplace would be an impediment to the effective management of the firm. (This argument, of course, implies that effective management requires a hostile working environment for women.) Even though Neiertz had originally supported the inclusion of colleague harassment, the general opposition to a more restrictive regulation forced the DMWR team to drop it from the final bill proposal. In a recent interview, Neiertz stated that she had no qualms about weakening the bill as long as a sexual harassment bill was put on the books (July 1993).

Another major demand of the feminist community had been to compel employers to take responsibility for sexual harassment. Since the mid-1980s, activists had argued that employers should confront sexual harassment because of its potential to reduce the productivity of firms while increasing their susceptibility to costly litigation. However, French businesses have no real financial incentive to take action against harassment because French lawsuits are filed less frequently and, when damages are awarded, they are slight. Further, between 1972 and 1989, only ten sexual harassment cases were taken to court (Hubert 1994, 12). Thus, the dynamics of the Romano-Germanic legal system in France and the resultant legal culture make it difficult for a litigation-centered approach to sexual harassment to have a strong punitive or deterrent effect.[17]

Throughout the parliamentary debates, there was little discussion of management's responsibility in dealing with the issue of sexual harassment within firms. Indeed, the new sexual harassment legislation makes no direct reference to employer responsibility.

Prevention has been a major demand of sexual harassment advocates. In both the 1985 and 1989 conferences on sexual harassment, advocates had argued that sexual harassment contributed to an unhealthy work environment (AVFT 1990; Zelensky and Gaussot 1986). Advocates, thus, insisted that it should be dealt with by

17. The dynamics of the French legal system and culture have minimized the extent to which anti-discrimination law in general is an effective policy instrument to strike down gender-based employment inequities (Mazur 1996).

business institutions such as the factory councils, the work inspectorate or the health and welfare committees or *Comité d'Hygiène de Sécurité et des Conditions de Travail* (CHSCT). Employers remained reluctant to adopt prevention programs. Consequently, the original 1992 bill proposed by the DMWR had included an article which suggested that the worker-run health and welfare committees (CHSCT) could, if they chose to, develop information and prevention campaigns on sexual harassment in the workplace.

This article was initially eliminated during the Senate debates. Members of CHSCT committees interviewed by the Senate had objected to this unwanted task and were uncertain of what would be expected from them (Serusclat 1992, 20–21). The Communist parliamentary group in the Senate had also argued against any additional duties being given to the already overloaded CHSCT. The CHSCT clause was reintroduced during a second reading of the bill in the National Assembly and was included in the final legislation (*Loi* no. 92–1179 du 2 novembre, 1992).

The final text did not specifically mention sexual harassment but instead prohibited "the abuse of authority through the use of sex in workplace relations." It was voted into law on 24 October 1992. The final vote reflected the bipartisan support for symbolic policy on sexual harassment. Only the Communists abstained, most likely because they had opposed adding more responsibilities to the already overloaded health and welfare committees. As a consequence, although France was the first member of the European Community to adopt specific legislation on sexual harassment, the new legislation failed to meet the standards set by EU policy in the 1991 Commission Recommendation and attached Code of Practice.

Post Formulation

The *loi Neiertz* did not come into effect until February 1993,[18] and, as of the summer of 1994, the article inserted in penal code reform was still not in force.[19] The Deputy Ministry designed and distributed a brochure on both new laws. The Equal Opportunities Unit in the European Commission also disseminated a practical guide to fighting sexual harassment in the workplace in 1993. The French guide, however, was not based on the European model.

18. *Circulaire d'application du 11 février 1993* (in Office of Women's Rights 1993, 9).

19. Although government officials had predicted that the penal code reform would be in force by 1993, its implementation was delayed until July 1994.

In June 1993, the newly downgraded Office of Women's Rights (OFW)[20] sponsored an implementation workshop on the new laws in Paris. The day-long session brought together women's rights administrators, labor inspectors, members of the AVFT, and trade union representatives from the CFDT. Run by ministry femocrats, the workshop emphasized the symbolic nature of the new laws while, at the same time, stressing the importance of the new legal definitions of sexual harassment as a tool to encourage prevention programs in firms.[21]

Much of the workshop covered the process by which firms, with the help of trade union delegates, women's rights and labor administrators, could develop prevention programs. Potential legal redress for victims was not discussed. As femocrat Catherine Laret-Bedel stated during the workshop, "we do not want to stress sanctions but prevention." Also, during the workshop it was made clear that government officials in the women's rights offices would look to the already overloaded and underfunded AVFT for advice and initiatives in implementing the new policy at the local level.

The new French policy on sexual harassment is very limited, essentially because few regard the enforcement of these new laws as an effective deterrent. Moreover, as earlier noted, the dynamics of the Romano-Germanic code law system will likely minimize the punitive damages and the overall potential for mitigating the problem. In 1993, employers appeared to be pursuing a new strategy of suing for libel the women who had accused management of sexual harassment along with the AVFT members who provided assistance to them. In two cases that summer, employers were pursuing defamation charges against women who sent formal letters to them alleging sexual harassment and requesting that action be taken against it. I attended the courtroom proceedings of these two cases and found that judges and prosecutors appeared ignorant of sexual harassment and its repercussions (21 July 1993). They displayed a greater concern for the potential for libel than the sexual harassment from which the women were demanding relief. Although the libel cases were eventually dismissed, AVFT members argued that they served to exacerbate the existing reluctance of harassment victims to come forward (Interviews, Marie-Victoire Louis and Sylvie Cromer July 1994). Combined with the lack of a supportive institutional

---

20. The ministry was demoted to this administrative rank in the Social Affairs Ministry following the Right's victory in parliamentary elections in March 1993.

21. I attended the workshop. For a written report of the proceedings, see Office of Women's Rights (1993).

environment for gender-based discrimination cases in general, litigation under the new laws will likely be minimal.

Conclusion

The European Community clearly played an important role in the introduction of this issue. Within the Member States, it subsidized conferences and other feminist group activities that contributed to defining sexual harassment as a public problem, and it helped generate pressure for government-sponsored solutions. In the 1985 conference, advocates like Yvette Fuillet made explicit reference to the EU's influence. Without the overtly international aspect of the 1989 conference, the apathetic Deputy Minister of Women's Rights may not have placed sexual harassment on the government agenda. Also, during the pre-formulation process, femocrats within the women's ministry used EU resolutions, declarations, and reports to strengthen their case for sexual harassment legislation to Michèle André. In 1991, when Véronique Neiertz definitively placed sexual harassment legislation on her government's decision agenda, supranational pressure from the impending Commission Recommendation helped the Deputy Minister to convince the more recalcitrant members of her government. Thus, in the formative (pre-formulation) stages of French policy, EU practices were used by governmental and nongovernmental advocates in France. The EU provided one political tool of many that legitimized and compelled the French state to take action against sexual harassment in the workplace.

Just as clearly, EU policy did little to influence the content and implementation of French legislation. The new French sexual harassment policy fails to follow even the general direction of the European Commission Recommendation and attached Code of Practice. This gap between French and European policy was partially a result of the absence of an authoritative EU policy instrument, like a directive or regulation, that legally obligated Member States to develop and implement a particular policy. The gap also resulted, in part, from the open hostility of policymakers outside of the women's rights ministries to decisive legislation.

In conclusion, European Union policy can have an influence in the pre-formulation stages of policymaking by helping advocates within Member States draw public attention to a particular issue. EU policy provides an additional reason for state decision makers to place controversial issues on their government and decision agendas. At the same time, unless European policy has direct authority, the scope of this supranational policy will be limited to symbolic reform, particularly in countries like France which have legal systems and political cultures that are not conducive to the legal approaches often contained in European directives. In the final analysis, EU policy will only be implemented if the most powerful policy actors within the Member States are so inclined.

4

PORNOGRAPHY AND SEXUAL HARASSMENT IN THE EU[1]

Susanne Baer

Sexual harassment, like pornography, is discrimination based on sex.[2] The former is legally recognized as such in the United States, the latter is not. Sexual harassment is recognized as sex discrimination by the institutions of the European Community and the Member States. Pornography is recognized as discriminatory in the labor market but is not recognized as doing harm to women. This incongruity results from a deficient understanding of discrimination and equality.

This chapter attempts to demonstrate that the inability of European law to respond properly to sexual discrimination is based in its incomprehension of what sexual harassment and pornography are in the world and what equality should be in the law. While United States law generally lacks this understanding as well, its law against sexual harassment and its concept of civil rights nevertheless offer starting points for conceptualizing adequate legal responses to sexual discrimination.

First, my argument centers on a comparative analysis of North American and European approaches to equality and its relation to the social universality of male dominance and sexual violence. Second, an analysis of European equality law evidences its inadequacy to react to this condition. Third, the new developments concerning a legal approach to sexual harassment and pornography in Europe illustrate that, despite the acceptance of a harm principle in liberal

1. Thanks go to Ulrich Baer for tremendous help, to Catharine A. MacKinnon for support, encouragement, and inspiration, and to Amy Elman for her thoughtful suggestions and the opportunity to present these ideas.
2. For a definition of pornography, see the ordinance by Dworkin and MacKinnon (1988, Appendix); for a definition of sexual harassment, see the decision in *Robinson v. Jacksonville Shipyards, Inc.*, 760 F. Supp. 1468 (M.D. Fla. 1991).

theory, harm to women does not yet constitute the basis of existing law. Fourth, this injustice may be addressed with a substantial concept and practice of nondiscrimination. This praxis, known as civil rights, developed in the African-American civil rights movement and has, more recently, been advanced to achieve feminist goals (MacKinnon, 1987; 1989; 1993). Finally, although comparative cross-cultural discourse should be pursued with caution, it provides us with inspirational paths towards rethinking the social and legal dimensions of equality. Our normative understandings of community and its characteristics, whether European, North American, or any other, correspond to specific historical, social, cultural, and legal experiences; equality, however, should be recognized as a universal claim.

Commonalities

Sexual violence is universal. Sexual violence affects distinct groups differently: women versus men, girls versus boys, women who belong to minorities versus those who are part of the dominant social group. However, this recognition of differences need not compromise the understanding of male dominance as pervasive.

Pornography, as discrimination on the basis of sex, violates women everywhere. Marketed throughout the world, pornography is not limited to the countries of its production, nor is the abuse of women through it limited to such locations. In some places, women are raped and tortured and killed for pictures; everywhere, women are silenced.

Differences can be found in the level of availability of pornography in different cultures, but that does not mean that most people cannot get what they want regardless of the abstract legal situation. Likewise, differences can be found in the level of acceptance of this form of sexual discrimination but not in its discriminatory nature as such.

Like pornography, sexual harassment is a worldwide practice (International Labour Organization 1992; Rubenstein 1988). More differences may exist between harassment in a factory and in a government office, for example, than between harassment in Germany and in the United States. The gender line which is constituted by sexual discrimination transcends national or cultural boundaries. The pervasiveness of sexual violence attaches reality to the theory that men and women are, as social beings, constituted by a gendered dynamic of dominance and subordination. Over time, attempts to quantify the ways in which men treat women as sexual objects at work and throughout life prove impossible. Generally, women are whistled at, verbally insulted, grabbed, punched, forcibly kissed, and sometimes raped. Everyday, many women have to look at pornography at work. It is in this last instance that sexual harassment and pornography physically coincide as sexual discrimination.

European Reaction to Inequalities

In Europe, sexual harassment is recognized when it happens to women in the wage labor market. It is, however, not legally recognized in the street, the home, or when it is part of the job, as in the pornography industry.[3] The European Community is concerned with employment to secure the functioning of the Common Market. The Community is an economically oriented entity, maybe more of a market than common. As a consequence, it recognizes the economic forms of exploitation more easily than other forms of discrimination. European institutions pay attention to wages, to labor conditions, and to the free movement of workers in the Union. The Union focuses its attention on differences based on nationality and sex only if these differences inhibit market growth.[4] The EU is concerned for men and women in their capacities as employees but not when subordination is marketed as a good to be bought and sold (see Leidholdt's chapter).

When exploitation does not have an obvious economic impact, the EU hardly responds. In March 1994, however, the European Secretaries for Women's Affairs adopted a resolution which emphasized violence against women as a serious threat to sex equality.[5] Nonetheless, this declaration is not legally binding.

Throughout Europe, women's movements as well as women in the political establishment have fought (and are still fighting) for a

3. The decision in the United States case of *Thoreson v. Guccione*, No.13039/81 (N.Y. County, 1990) provides an exception. Being prostituted and used in pornography was regarded as actionable under Human Rights Law. See also Bowman (1993) and the newer development of laws against stalking.

4. See Articles 48 and 117 of the EC Treaty and the Preamble to the Single European Act. Generally, see Ellis (1991, 62, 209); Fredman (1992, 119–134); Prechal and Burrows (1990). Usually, such analyses do not cover sexual violence.

5. Final Resolution from the Conference on the political and social situation of women in Europe towards the year 2000, Brussels. Information-Bulletin from German Minister of Women and Youth, 7 March 1994, No. 14.

recognition of pornography and sexual harassment as gender inequalities. However, reality remains essentially unchanged. One reason is that sex equality as a right is anchored in Article 119 of the EC Treaty which promises to promote sex equality only within the confines of the labor market (Hoskyns 1992).[6]

An additional reason for EU's limited response to sexual inequality is that Article 119 is interpreted in a formal (i.e., an Aristotelian), symmetrical manner. The issue, it is said, is difference, not disadvantage or dominance. As far as gender is concerned, what is biological or crucial to the functioning of society is termed a difference which has to be accommodated. In legal doctrine, such a difference is a formal inequality which may be justified. The social formation of differences, including those which may be biologically based, is ignored. The differences, be they advantageous or disadvantageous, are not undone. Generally, for women, these differences are detrimental. The more women are different from men, the less equality works for them.[7] In addition, the focus is either on the individual or a group complete with no exceptions. "Equality" so conventionally conceived ignores the distinct and multifaceted characteristics of collectives and the different ways of belonging to them. When formal equality is applied, one compares equally situated individuals or groups within a hierarchical status quo; one neither intends nor allows for the possibility to change it.

In the European Community, as in the world, human rights law treats equality the same way. For example, Article 14 of the European Convention for the Protection of Human Rights and Fundamental Freedoms guarantees that such rights "shall be secured without discrimination" on many grounds, including gender. In this context, equality is interpreted not only symmetrically, but also as a

6. In addition, there is a general but weak principle of sex equality for employees of the Community itself. See *Razzouk and Beydoun v. Commission* Cases 75 and 117/82 [1984] ECR 1509. Also note Catherine Hoskyns's chapter in this volume.

7. For example, *Hertz* Case 179/88 [1990] ECR 3879. It was held that although maternity leave is obligatory, a dismissal due to sickness due to pregnancy can only be justified on the the basis of similar laws for men. In *Integrity* Case 373/89 [1991] IRLR 176, men gained benefits reserved for women, widows, and students. The problem of benign versus invidious discrimination is also exemplified in *Hofmann v. Barmer Ersatzkasse* Case 184/83 [1984] ECR 3047, where maternity leave is granted only for mothers, and *Bilka-Kaufhaus GmbH v. Weber Von Hartz* Case 170/84 [1986] ECR 1607, according to which employers do not have to accommodate the needs of women with families. See generally Prechal and Burrows (1990). For the theoretical critique of the formal approach to equality, see MacKinnon (1989), especially Chapter 12.

complementary and sometimes subsidiary guarantee of the free-doms in the Convention. For example, the Court did not approach equality from the context of rape or abortion nor did it address the ways in which gay men's social families are destroyed by states.[8] Thus, European human rights law does not recognize a substantial right to equality on its own terms.

The European situation however is not unique. Law in the United States also works with this symmetrical version of equality. Only Canada has been moved beyond it and applied equality doctrine to sexual violence.[9] In Germany, the Federal Constitutional Court announced in 1992 that sex equality is a right to transform social subordination into equality but has yet to recognize sexual violence as a version of such subordination.[10] In the United States, the law against sexual harassment is the one exception to the otherwise for-mal rule. There, sexual hierarchy is noticed as inequality. Women (or men, if they suffer sex-based injustice) may bring sex discrimi-nation suits against harassers and their employers and courts adju-dicate remedies ranging from back pay to injunctions.[11]

In the United States, sexual harassment law covers specific appear-ances of pornography but not pornography as such (*Robinson v. Jacksonville Shipyards, Inc.* 1991). Recently, there have been efforts to destroy the progress made toward substantive sex equality. These attempts have been based on a right to freedom of speech for men, but they have not been successful (MacKinnon 1993). Sexual harass-ment remains—legally and socially—a recognized inequality done to women. Pornography in the world, however, remains "a moral issue," which, as Catharine A. MacKinnon once stated, it is not

8. In appl. No. 9369/81, *x. v. UK* [1981] 5 EHRR 501, England denied a Malay-sian the right to live with his lover because it did not recognize gay men as "family" or a gay man as a "wife." The Court failed to examine the implications surrounding a sex-specific dependency requirement or the implicit norm of heterosexuality. For remedies in rape cases see *x. and y. v. Netherlands* (Series A., No. 91) [1986] EHRR 235, 26 March 1985. On abortion, see *Open Door Counseling and Dublin Well Woman v. Ireland* (Series A., No. 246) [1992] 15 EHRR 244, 29 October 1992. For an equality perspective, see Olsen (1989) and MacKinnon (1991).

9. For a discussion of equality in general, note *The Law Society of British Colum-bia v. Andrews* [1989] 1.S.C.R. 143; on pornography in particular, read *Butler v. Regina* (1991), 2. W.W.R. 557.

10. The decision declared the prohibition of night shifts as unconstitutional, BVer-fGe (Sammlung der Entscheidungen des Bundesverfassungsgerichts Band) 85, 191, 207; a subsequent decision held that equality also guarantees access for women to men's jobs, Bundesverfassungsgericht in: STREIT 1994, 126.

11. On the state of the law, see Lindemann and Kadue (1992); for the analysis, MacKinnon (1979).

(1987, 146–162). In European as well as United States law, pornography is considered obscene, not harmful; speech, not propaganda; thought, not act. It is not, thus, understood as discrimination. A morality approach sustains the dominant order. Therefore and until now, law has not done much against pornography.[12] An inequality approach, not yet accepted, intends to change it.

Recent European Developments

With regard to sexual harassment and pornography, there have been new developments in the European Community. On a social level, protectively cloaked within a rhetoric of freedom, the buying and selling of women increased and pornography has flooded large parts of Eastern Europe. On the other hand, consciousness has been raised about sexual discrimination in employment. This enhanced understanding may have resulted from the attention former socialist countries extended to women in employment.

On a legal level, activities against sexual harassment have rapidly proliferated since 1988 (see Collins' chapter). That year, British lawyer Michael Rubenstein presented a requested study on sexual harassment in the EC and suggested anti-discrimination law against it (1988). At the same time, Sweden issued its first report on sexual harassment at work (Hagmann 1992). In 1990, the European Council decided to recommend action (OJ C 157/3, 27 June 1990). However, the Council did not analyze sexual harassment as sex-based discrimination but as a violation of men's and women's dignity. Dignity is wonderful. In post-Kantian philosophy and in the German constitution, dignity is the principle which governs all individual rights. It gained particular importance after World War II when it was emphasized as a human right in order to prevent forever a repetition of the Nazi atrocities of the Holocaust. However, the concept of dignity is individualistic, not collective, gender-neutral, not gender-sensitive, egalitarian, not anti-hierarchical.

Some might argue that a right to human dignity prohibits discrimination. From this perspective, discrimination is not regarded as a pervasive part of the social fabric. Others may hold that dignity is the reference point of equality, the *tertium comparationis* needed by the Aristotelian interpretation. In this instance, discrimination

---

12. An exception may be child pornography. See *New York v. Ferber*, 458 U.S. 747 (1982).

cannot be seen as a group-based process because dignity is a fundamentally individual claim. Socially, however, dignity is a part of equality: you have dignity when you are equal. Dignity without equality does not exist.

In 1991, the EU and its Member States initiated measures against sexual harassment in employment. The European Commission issued a Code of Practice on Measures to Combat Sexual Harassment (OJ L 49/1, 24 February 1992);[13] France created a combination of criminal and labor law measures (Mazur 1993);[14] Germany adopted its "workers protection law" in 1994. Again, all these efforts center on dignity, not equality. The German law defines harassment as intentional behavior, thus shifting the focus of inquiry to a man's mind and ignoring the harm that is, or should be, the basis for legal intervention. In law against discrimination, the intent requirement is illegal under EC law.[15] Ignoring this and retaining a focus on individual dignity, sexual harassment law in Germany is destined to be ineffective from its inception.

Despite the numerous obstacles to effective redress, the EC triggered legal action towards sex equality. From the perspective of the Member States, it was not the first time (Fredman 1992; McGinley 1986, 425–427). But it was the first time that the Community acted, however ineffectively, to counter an overtly sexualized form of sex discrimination.

With regard to pornography, it is recognized officially as harmful and a violation of dignity when it constitutes part of sexual harassment in employment. It is as if such harassment can be considered discriminatory only in employment.[16] The only European institution to conclude differently is the European Parliament, which issued a resolution on pornography in December 1993.[17] Convinced that the victims of pornography are entitled to protection, the Parliament has urged the Member States to take legal action against it. This European institution views pornography as "a

13. The Commission wanted to ensure that sexual harassment be seen as discrimination. See also the explanation provided by Rubenstein (in European Commission 1993).

14. Note also Christine Delphy's cautionary remarks concerning France in this volume.

15. Note *Dekker v. Stichting Vormingscentrum Voor Jonge Volwassen Plus* Case 177/88 [1991] IRLR 27.

16. Legal recognition is otherwise focused on the protection of youth and the regulation of TV and broadcasting (Guideline 89/552/EEC, 10 October 1989, Art. 12, 16, 22). Note the Dutch reservation to allow for pornography channels at night.

17. Protocol, EP, 17 December 1993, PV 50, PE 177.124; 57.

systematic practice of exploitation and subordination on the basis of sex, which disadvantages women ... and contributes to the inequality of the sexes, the already existing unequal power structures in society, female subordination, and male dominance."[18]

In addition, the Parliament observed an increasing presence of pornography in the world which causes behavior that is particularly damaging to women and children, whether they are used in it or whether it is used upon them.[19] The Parliament is an exception to European ignorance, yet it is relatively powerless. This powerlessness might, on some level, contribute to its exceptional ability to comprehend the reality of women's lives.

Despite the efforts taken by the European Parliament to convince Europe of pornography's harm, neither the Commission nor the Council nor the Court shares or accepts the analysis that pornography is subordination.[20] Member States do not possess a clear definition of pornography, nor have they implemented any substantive prohibitions. Indeed, some states, like Germany, Portugal, and France, make money from taxing such trafficking in women.[21]

There are three essential reasons why the European Union reacts to sexual harassment differently than it does to pornography. First, in cases of sexual harassment in employment, economic and sexual exploitation more clearly coincide. The general economic focus of European law thus enabled the institutions to grasp the severity of the problem. Note that the United States based its Civil Rights Act on the Commerce Clause, which is also a market-oriented provision. In the United States, however, law against sexual harassment

---

18. Protocol, P. 59 (K.) Sections 5. A., 5. B., 13., 14. My translation from German. See also the Report of the Committee on Freedoms and Internal Affairs (Jean-Thomas Nordemann), 24 September 1993; DOC-DE\RR\237287. PE 204, 592. The Nordemann report includes the findings and arguments which led to the Protocol and a listing of the legal situation in all Member States.

19. It was noted that the women used in pornography shall be protected through combatting sexual violence and through, at the same time, offering protection as well as options to "sex industry workers" to get out. This is consistent with the European approach to prostitution, which is, in the abstract, legal as long as it is not exploitative. Realistically, then, it cannot be legal. See Leidholdt in this volume for an analysis of prostitution, and Dworkin and MacKinnon (1988) on protection for women who "work" in pornography.

20. Note that the Council urged "adequate sanctions" on child pornography R (91) 11, and compare the report by Lissy Gröner, Appendix II to the Nordemann Report, supra n. 20, at 27–32.

21. See the Nordemann Report, supra n. 20, at 21.

became equality oriented; under Title VII, a successful claim need not include proof of economic loss.

Second, in cases of sexual harassment in employment, the abuse transcends the "private sphere" in ways that make it explicitly violative. Moreover, when sexual abuse interferes with an area of economic interest, it surpasses the obstacles of hypocrisy usually applied to cases of discrimination. Thus, in the case of harassment, a legal reaction was possible. At the same time, the pornography which might be discrimination at work remains untouched as long as it is used in private.[22]

Third, European legal inactivity against sexual abuse in the form of pornography is legitimated by European courts. In 1979, the Court of Justice decided that a state cannot prohibit the import of pornography if it does not ban the production itself (*Conegate Ltd.* 1986).[23] In this area, even critical commentators find that "juggling the values of equality, morality, the public good, and a Single European Market" will be difficult (Clapham 1991, 26 n. 49). The Court, in an earlier case (*Handyside* 1976), held that national authorities are best able to adjudicate changing opinions on the subject because they are in closest touch with "the vital forces of their countries."[24] This argument implies that equality is a culturally relative claim and that Europe, as a whole, should not then act against pornography.

Considering the absence of implementation of any law in this area, it seems that authorities and institutions have sided with male interests. Criminal or public obscenity laws against pornography have long proven ineffective because they empower the state, not victims of discrimination, to take in/action. This lesson was learned by Norwegian feminists who, after years of organizing, had a law

22. Note Appl. No. 10461/83, *Chappell v. United Kingdom*, ECHR, A No. 152, 30 March 1989, in which the search of a video club owner's home was considered legal for copyright reasons, while it was not important that the videos were pornographic. His "private" life would have been protected by Article 8 of the Convention. Socially, this protects sexual violence at home, not women. Compare Ronald Dworkin (1985, 335–372).

23. *Regina v. Henn and Darby* Case 34/79 [1979] ECR 3795 (Danish pornography into UK); *Conegate Limited v. HM Customs & Excise* Case 121/85; Judgment of 11 March 1986 (inflatable rubber dolls imported into UK); *Quietlynn and Richards v. Southbend Borough Council* Case 23/89; Judgment of 11 July 1990 (a national prohibition to sell sex articles in unlicensed stores does not interfere with EC law as long as such things can be sold elsewhere).

24. *Handyside* Case, Judgment of 7 December 1976, Series A No. 24, 1 EHHR 737. See also Appl. No. 10737/84, *Müller and others v. Switzerland*, 24 May 1988, Series A No. 133, 13 EHRR 212 (conviction of artist for obscene art upheld).

adopted that the authorities then failed to implement.[25] Authorities in the Member States have not yet pursued women's equality.

Equality Against Discrimination

What, then, would blunt sex discrimination? What would law and life have to look like, what would equality mean, and what is a community, European or otherwise, without discrimination?

When considered in detail, the European legal developments against sexual harassment, however promising, are not equipped with the legal force they need: the Union issued a recommendation, for example, not a directive.[26] Moreover, when transformed into national law, the Recommendation takes a traditional liberal and state-oriented form. Consequently, such measures may offer some protection, not freedom and equality. National European laws against sexual harassment are not civil rights laws. However, while the latter may provide for substantive notions of equality, they are no guarantee of justice.

In practice, the concept of civil rights is derived distinctively from the United States. Framed by the African-American liberation movement, they later became part of the feminist agenda in the United States. Within both movements, the use of rights is a profoundly political act. The procedure to secure such rights may be taken by individuals but without individualizing the claim. Any case moves against discrimination as an individually manifested *collective* disadvantage.

Civil rights against pornography and sexual harassment require the recognition of these harms as discrimination. Pornography would then, legally, be treated as discrimination based on sex and recognized by the harm it does. Women, in possession of civil rights, would be able to assert that they had been injured through pornography. They could mitigate the harm and be compensated for its occurrence (Dworkin and MacKinnon 1988). Sexual harassment would be approached in a similar manner—as discrimination based on sex, recognized by the harm it does. As with those harmed by

25. An exception seems to be sexist advertisements which may be illegal under trade and sex equality law; *Consumer Ombudsman v. Jegerhallen and Olav Thon* Case 10/81 Markedsradet (Norwegian Marketing Court) [1982] ECC 335, 9 October 1981.

26. The Parliament, not equipped with enough power to change it, issued critique of this decision, 11 February 1994 (EP-Doc. A3–43/94).

pornography, the victims of sexual harassment would have rights to compensation. Equality thus advanced is a right against dominance based on gender and ethnicity. It incorporates a concept of anti-subordination (MacKinnon, 1979, 1989, 1991).[27] Contrary to traditional interpretation, this approach to equality does not object to difference as long as it is not social and hierarchical. This anti-subordination approach is based on the analysis that in law, politics, and theory, differences are already recognized and that such recognition is oftentimes a part of discrimination (MacKinnon 1989). For the sake of brevity, equality as a right against discrimination is meant to produce a community quite different from the one we see when we look at Europe, or for that matter, the world.

History, Culture, Politics, and Comparison

There are many reasons why a civil rights-based approach to inequality (i.e., one which invokes an anti-hierarchical right to equality) is rarely used and frequently misunderstood or misapplied. European states do not allow for the simple transplantation of a civil rights approach so customary in the United States. A comparative perspective attempts to highlight some of the reasons and thus also to provide a basis for cross-national understanding, which, in a feminist epistemological context, is a mode for action (Baer 1994).

One previously noted explanation for the dearth of civil rights approaches to pornography and sexual harassment is that, legally, European institutions and governments regard equality as symmetrical difference. Thus, as long as equality is not a substantive guarantee against hierarchies, but a formal threshold against any difference which cannot be justified—as in most European and U.S. jurisdictions—law will not care who suffers from discrimination. If equality is a principle preserving an already unjust status quo, not a remedial right against injustice, European as well as U.S. law will lag behind Canadian jurisprudence.

A second reason is historical. Europe has a very specific political background and legal culture. Its national histories include monarchy, totalitarianism, and a strongly developed bureaucracy. In European societies, the state is much stronger than in those cultures

27. Compare the weaker versions of MacKinnon's approach, coined the "disadvantage principle" by Rhode (1989), Sunstein's version (1992), and the groundbreaking work by Fiss (1976).

unaccustomed to high levels of state intervention. Structurally and historically, a "strong" state is expected to pursue social equality. From the perspective of the disadvantaged, this pursuit proves disappointing, yet the political reaction is often to plead for further state action, not less. Again, the expectation is that the state will deliver on its promises. Reliance on the state was, in part, practiced by Norwegian women in their fight against pornography. Similarly, rather than pursue a civil rights approach against pornography, German and Swedish feminists expected state action. They were disappointed.[28] Reliance on the state in majoritarian political systems is not a sound strategy if subordination is practiced and legitimized on a mass scale. Also, political systems which center on strong political parties tend to exclude the needs of those who never gain significant access into the political system. Legislation—which feminists often proposed—may help, but litigation and activism must shape its implementation. Lobbying legislative bodies is, thus, one of the most desperately needed forms of activism.

A more current examination of European states provides a third explanation. Most of the nation states that comprise the EU have civil law systems; Ireland and England are more peculiar cases. At present, civil law does not differ much from common law with regard to regulation, but culturally, a primarily legislative and governmental civil law system produces a legal conscience which is not, as in liberal common law states, centered on individually enforced rights. In the United States, rights are used against, besides, and without the state. "Having your day in court" is welcomed. Litigation is both a highly individualized and political means to change policy. Women's rights groups side with litigants and possess some option of class action. In using law against discrimination, North Americans tend to assert their status as citizens. For Europeans, existing law is supposed to grant one that status. This, in part, explains why the European welfare states are, relative to the United States, more advanced and differently developed. But, broadly speaking, it also means that Europeans may wait for the state forever and never have "their day" anywhere. Waiting for the state, then, is waiting for legislation, which requires greater collective effort and produces more political compromise than the individual act of bringing a case.

---

28. For the case of Sweden, see *Pornografi: Verklighet eller Fantasi* (1991); for Germany, see Dane and Schmidt (1990) and for a proposed civil rights law against pornography in Germany, see Baer and Slupik (1988).

Fundamentally, North American common law systems are not without disadvantages, and European civil law systems have a specific value of their own. If, for example, "rights talk" disempowers a political, community-oriented, and discursive process, more individual rights may be detrimental to society in the long run (Glendon 1991). Continental legislative systems offer advantages. Legislative change provides for more stability in law than jurisprudential developments. Legislation also tends to be seen as a more democratic process when compared to court rulings. That is exactly one critique leveled against progressive EU law, which, unlike most national law, is primarily shaped by litigation. However, in traditionally legislative schemes dominating Europe, the democratic value of courts tends to be overlooked.

Both continental and common law seem to offer important elements for securing rights to sex (and other) equality. Political and legal strategies that attempt to avoid both individualism as well as state reliance may perhaps be revealed through an examination of other systems. The Canadian and Japanese systems provide two examples which should be examined further as both contain a mix of civil and common law traditions.

There is a fourth, more complex, and tentative explanation why sexual equality is lacking in law and community. It raises the importance of perceptions. European standards of relative social security imply that the potential for equality already exists and that, as many liberal theorists held, over the course of modernity, inequality will vanish entirely. This perception obscures sex discrimination. Moreover, the fact that most European societies are less pervaded by visible physical violence than the United States tends to remove sexual violence far from public view. Lastly, in many places sexual violence has not yet been thoroughly and adequately documented.

A candid comparative discussion of sexual politics in the United States and Europe would be remiss to overlook the European fear of U.S. prudery. This anxiety is, in part, ideologically maintained. For example, feminist efforts against pornography and sexual harassment in the United States are either suppressed and/or caricatured as an embodiment of declining Western culture, the horror image of what can happen if one goes "too far." In these images, feminists are portrayed as excessively moralistic, rigid, shrink-infested, anti-sex fanatics—an image Europeans are expected to detest. In consequence, sophisticated Europeans are reluctant to support feminist efforts to end sexual subordination. In addition, European reporting sometimes replicates the widespread inaccuracies contained in

U.S. accounts of feminism. For example, political commentators will insist on alliances between right-wing politicians and feminists that do not exist, a tactic often invoked to delegitimize women's fight against pornography in particular. Such analyses ignore the ways in which feminism sought to unmask the hypocrisy of conservatism which has failed to discern pornography as sexual discrimination. Conservative lawmaking does not intend to put remedial means in the hands of victims *and* end all women's inequality. Feminism is to prudery what water is to fire. In Europe, however, false reporting of North American feminism is used to denigrate the fight for sex equality.

The fifth and final reason for the conceptual limitations on civil rights rest on the socio-historical nature of Europe. Based upon a distinction between immigrant groups and minorities, this explanation is also tentative. European nation-states have not been and are not formed by immigrants in the way the United States and Canada are. In both countries, immigrants construct these cultures rather than comprising a less important part of them. Also, immigrants typically have an experience of what it means to be different, to be disliked, a foreigner, unwelcome when they arrive. In addition, many experienced inequality in the places they left behind. Immigrants often know what discrimination is, and, as a consequence, a heightened sense of tolerance and individualistic pluralism may form a greater part of their culture. That is not to say, however, that the United States and Canada are without racism, cultural bias, homophobia, and sexism. In both states, these prevailing conditions are evidence of the need to go further. In Europe, however, societies are not comprised of immigrants but of dominant groups and minorities. Religious minorities played an especially important role in the development of the notion of tolerance and liberalism. However, minorities form distinct groups within a society that are either isolated or forced to assimilate.

In the context of discrimination, the difference between immigrant and majority-minority cultures (which certainly is a simplification) has important legal and theoretical consequences. A majority-minorities society is based on a perception that there are either groups (e.g., "them") or individuals (e.g., "we"), but there are no individuals who comprise different groups. Therefore, law reacts to groups or individuals, but not to discrimination as a practice of targeting an individual for being part of a group. Opposed to this, the immigrant society of the United States is based on the perception that there are only individuals or one big group (e.g.,

"Americans").[29] Therefore, law does not organize the broader social response to inequality, as in European welfare states, but offers individual means to justice.

A Community for All

The formation of the European Community has been inspired by a "European idea." It embodies the idea of peace and of freedom, based on growth and welfare rather than pluralist equality. The Community itself has produced a need to better understand pluralism. The rapidly changing nature of European societies, as well as the European Community, demands that hierarchies be considered sensible. Danes and Norwegians protested the hierarchy between Brussels and Copenhagen or Oslo.[30] Many other hierarchies are increasingly more obvious at every moment. Civil rights and substantive equality could help to undo them. A community that wants to remain true to the spirit of community will have to address this. To consider the human rights of women within a European constitution is one step, but it will not help women or other people discriminated against if equality remains as weak as it is now under the Convention. To develop a European social policy is one step, but it will not help if discrimination is not properly understood and if the symmetrical understandings of difference are not abandoned.

Feminists, it seems, are ahead in understanding these dynamics. So, too, are other anti-hierarchical movements and thinkers. But, if equality does not become more than an inspirational idea of this political minority, Europe will be a very difficult place in which to live for many. If equality is not made real, a community cannot be either. After all, a community—be it the United States, Europe, or elsewhere—is unthinkable without an end to discrimination, sexual or any other.

29. The hegemonic aspect of this term excludes Latin and Middle America as well as Canada. Native peoples as well as, for example, the Inuit are often overlooked.
30. See Hoskyns's note 12 concerning the Scandinavian opposition.

❧ 5

PORNOGRAPHY, HARM, AND HUMAN RIGHTS
The UK in European Context

Catherine Itzin

This chapter begins with an overview of the harm done to women in and through pornography. It discusses the current status of obscenity law in the United Kingdom and how it conflicts with European Community law. The article concludes with a consideration of existing UK sex and race discrimination law as well as UN and European instruments which could provide redress to women across European frontiers.

The Social Status of Women[1]

In the UK, women are economically subordinate in relation to men. They are largely to be found in low-paid, low-status, sex-segregated work, and increasingly in part-time work. Women's earnings are still only three-quarters of men's earnings, and there has been very little change in the gap between women's and men's earnings in the twenty years since the Equal Pay and Sex Discrimination Acts were implemented (Equal Opportunities Commission 1993). Women are also routinely the objects of physical, emotional, and sexual violence perpetrated by men. In the UK, the police receive over a million calls a year from women who are the victims of violence by known men. "Domestic violence" comprises 25 percent of all assaults recorded by the police (British Crime Statistics 1989). Given the notable reluctance of women to report the violence men perpetrate against them, the real numbers are certainly higher. In

---

1. All the statistics in this paper refer to the UK unless otherwise stated. They will, however, be comparable to those in other Western industrialized states.

1991, ten million women in the UK reported receiving obscene telephone calls. Hall (1985) recorded a prevalence of 21 percent for rape, and Beattie (1992) found 20 percent of a sample of 1,040 women students to have been victims of rape. The incidence of reported rape rises every year (Home Office Criminal Statistics 1985–1994), and most rape is not reported (Beattie 1992). Sometimes women are murdered just because they are women (Radford and Russell 1992).

On the basis of all available information, it is difficult not to conclude that women experience a great deal of harm on a routine day-to-day basis in the form of systematic economic and social subordination, as well as gender-based sexual violence and abuse. In order for this to happen, there must be a belief that it is permissible for women to be treated in this way: a message that women can be hurt and hit and hated and held in contempt and treated as less than human. One of the places that this message is communicated is in and through pornography.

The Status of Women in Pornography

In currently available commercial pornography, women are reduced to their genitals and anuses, posed open and gaping, inviting sexual access and penetration, presented as constantly sexually available, insatiable and voracious, or passive and servile, servicing men sexually. This is the standard content of most of the seventy-three "top shelf" titles sold in UK newsagents in the main ("high") streets of neighborhoods throughout the UK. High street newsagents also sell "specialist" magazines devoted to sexual violence (e.g., a woman masked and chained, her genitals exposed, another in dog collar and leather straps, legs trussed up like a chicken ready for stuffing). Common to all of this material is the portrayal of women as enjoying being raped, sexually abused, and humiliated (Russell 1993a). This is the material that sells legally in the UK (Itzin 1992).

Illegal material, from under the counter in London's red light district (Soho) and specialist sex shops elsewhere, is also easily available. The Obscene Publications Branch at Scotland Yard has seized material which includes a woman having her labia nailed to the top of a table and needles being inserted into nipples and genitals (Itzin 1992). Material in which women are shown having sex with animals is easily available in the UK (Itzin and Wingfield 1992). There is also evidence of a market in snuff films where women are sexually murdered on camera (Corcoran 1989; Itzin 1992). Users of pornography may describe their experience as "fantasy," but real women and children are used in the production of pornography where the evidence of harm is visible (Kappeler 1986, 1992; Kelly and O'Hara 1990).

There is now a very substantial body of evidence that women are harmed through the making and the use of pornography. This harm includes sexual murder, rape, sexual assault, sexual harassment, coercion into the use of pornography, and sexual objectification. Simply put, pornography contributes to women's subordinate status in society. The evidence takes different forms: clinical studies and research with sex offenders, social science and psychological research, and the testimony of the many survivors of sexual abuse, both in and outside the pornography industry, who have given first-hand accounts of the harm they have experienced by and through pornography (Malamuth and Check 1983; Russell 1988; Wyre 1992; Zillmann and Weaver 1989). The academic research is corroborated by sex offender evidence and the testimony of women; and conversely, real-life experience is corroborated by academic research. Taken together, the various evidence points in the same direction—toward the links between the manufacture and use of violent and subordinating pornography and different kinds of harm to women.

All this material is sold as "sex" for the "entertainment" of men. It is seen as sex because it is sexually explicit and because it elicits sexual arousal and orgasm. In the sexualized context of pornography, the dehumanization and subordination of so-called soft core pornography and the violence and torture of women in "hard core" pornography are not recognized as such. The routine sexualizing and reinforcement of racist stereotypes and racism are similarly ignored (Collins 1993; Forna 1992; Mayall and Russell 1993).

Incitement to Hatred and Violence

Another dimension to the harm of pornography is its function as a form of incitement to sexual hatred and violence. Words and images of anti-Semitism and race hatred have been used to incite hatred and violence against Blacks and Jews. Words have, as Catharine A. MacKinnon (1993) has argued, the power to harm. Race hate propaganda has been used to enable and normalize routine practices of violence and abuse, discrimination, and extermination. For Black people, incitement to racial hatred and violence has meant lynching, slavery, and segregation in the United States, and violent attacks and murder on the street in the UK: just for being Black. For European Jews, the propaganda of anti-Semitism was instrumental to their torture and extermination by the Nazis in the Holocaust. For women, the propaganda of misogyny underpins economic, social and sexual subordination, exploitation, violence, and abuse so routine as to be regarded as unremarkable, even normal.

Amnesty International is an organization which campaigns against the imprisonment and torture of people on political grounds and for the human rights of people who are so treated. In the UK, Amnesty recruits support with full-page advertisements in national newspapers, often using pictures of political prisoners being tortured. When the Amnesty International pictures of political torture are compared with those of women being tortured in pornography, it is difficult to see any difference from a human rights perspective. But one significant difference is that pornography is sold—and seen by most people—*not* as violence and torture, but as sex. In the UK, you cannot go into newsagents and buy racist and anti-Semitic caricatures of Black people and Jews, but you can purchase the sexualized violence and abuse of women in pornography where the harm has apparently become invisible. The harm to women in and through pornography is neither perceived nor acknowledged.

The Pornography Industry

A major difference between pornography and the political torture which Amnesty campaigns against is that the sexual violence, violation, and torture of women in pornography is part of a multibillion pound international industry (Baxter 1990). It was estimated that the so-called "top shelf soft porn" magazines would sell "over twenty million copies" in the UK in 1990 and be read by about "five million people"—mostly men (Baxter 1990, 37). Another source put the total sales of British monthly pornography magazines at 2.25 million copies, pointing out that these were only estimates because large segments of the industry do not release sales figures (Cohen 1989). It was also estimated that several companies in Europe secured multimillion-pound turnovers on pornographic magazines and videos in 1990 (Baxter 1990, 37).

In the United States, the majority of the pornography industry is run by organized crime (Attorney General's Commission 1986). In

Britain, pornography is produced by respected members of the mainstream publishing industry. Paul Raymond, publisher of *Men Only* and owner of the Soho Strip Club, Raymonds Revue Bar, also has extensive property holdings in Soho and was recently listed as one of the wealthiest men in England (Cowe 1993). Northern and Shell publish *Fitness, Green Magazine, Stamps,* and *Bicycle* as well as *Penthouse,* and Prince Philip recently fronted a high profile launch of the opening of their new offices (Picardie 1993, 14–16). *Company* and *Cosmopolitan* are distributed by the same company as *Penthouse.* And, until it ceased publication, the same firm also distributed *Spare Rib,* a British feminist journal. *Women's World* is printed on the same presses as *Men Only.*

Governmental and Judicial Findings

In 1989, 112 members of the British parliament from all parties put forward an Early Day Motion expressing "grave concern about the continued rise in sales, both covert and overt, of pornographic and obscene material." Noting that "such publications have a grossly degrading and damaging effect, particularly in their depiction of women and children" and "the increasingly extreme cruelty and violence involved in such material," the Motion stated "that the anecdotal evidence is now overwhelming that this kind of stimulus is an important factor in encouraging criminal acts affecting innocent victims" and called "on Her Majesty's Government to initiate an urgent study of the impact of pornography to update and supplement the limited research currently available and thereafter to implement urgently whatever measures are necessary to protect those who directly or indirectly suffer as a result of such perverting influences" (*Hansard,* Notices of Motions, 21 November 1989, No. 1, 11).[2] The Home Office responded by commissioning a review of the existing research relating to pornography. It concluded that there was no evidence of any causal links between pornography and sexual violence (Howitt and Cumberbatch 1990, 84).

The results of the Home Office review have been rigorously challenged by women's organizations and by leading international pornography researchers (Itzin 1994). The conclusions of the report were, however, consistent with the previously published views of its

---

2. One may note that the acknowledged sufferers do not include those in the pornography.

authors. In 1979, they had given evidence to the Williams Committee on Obscenity and Film Censorship that the "mass media—as far as it is possible to tell using social scientific methodologies—do not serve to amplify the level of violence in society" (Williams Committee Report 1979, 67). In the same year that the Home Office commissioned their review of the research relating to pornography, they had published a report commissioned by the Broadcasting Standards Council on the effects of pornography in which they concluded that "there does not seem to be compelling and unequivocal evidence that allows any strong conclusion about pornography based on research" (BSC 1989, 77). They concluded in their BSC report that there was not "one jot of evidence which links this type of research finding with real-life sexual violence" (Cumberbatch and Howitt 1989, 72). At the time, their views had been widely published in the national press (Cohen 1989).

The evidence of pornography-related harm has been accepted, however, by governments in the United States (Department of Justice 1986), Canada (Fraser Commission 1985), Australia (*Report of the Joint Select Committee on Video Material* 1988), and New Zealand (*Pornography: Report of the Ministerial Committee of Inquiry* 1989). A Federal Appellate Court in the United States in 1985 found that

> Pornography is central in creating and maintaining sex as a basis for discrimination. Pornography is a systematic practice of exploitation and subordination based on sex which differentially harms women. The bigotry and contempt it produces, with the acts of aggression it fosters, harm women's opportunities for equality and rights of all kinds.

But the court decided that this "simply demonstrates the power of pornography as speech" and ruled that the free speech rights of the pornography industry took precedence over women's rights to be free of sexual violence and inequality (*American Booksellers Inc. v William H. Hudnut* 1985). When the harm is made visible, it is defended by libertarians as freedom of sexually explicit speech (Feminist Anti-Censorship Taskforce 1985).

Obscenity Legislation

There is currently no legislation against pornography in the UK. There is only legislation against obscenity and indecency. In 1979, the Williams Committee on Obscenity and Film Censorship concluded that the law was "a mess" (Williams Committee Report

1979, 20). It still is. Those in the criminal justice system, including ScotlandYard's Obscene Publications Squad, now regard the law as "unworkable," "unenforceable," "untenable," "unscientific," "illogical," "unpredictable," and as that which "provides a formula which cannot in practice be applied" (Robertson 1979, 7). According to a Labour MP seeking a debate on pornography in the House of Commons in 1992: "The public has been led to believe that our obscenity laws are strong. In fact they are a mess" (*Hansard*, Ms. Lynne, 2 July 1992, 1062).

This is partly because the definition of obscenity as material "likely to deprave and corrupt" is vague and subjective and open to such a variety of interpretation as to be meaningless. It is concerned with morality, whereas the problem with pornography is its harmful effects on women as a result of its manufacture and use. The UK Obscene Publications Act of 1959 is concerned with the "corrupting influence" of pornography on a "significant proportion" of "persons who are likely to read, see, or hear the matter" (Robertson 1979, 46). This formulation was based on the assumption that pornography only had a "corrupting" effect on a small minority of "deviant" dirty old men. This is contradicted by the evidence that pornography has negative effects on the attitudes and behavior of all the "normal," "ordinary" men who use it, and that it has particularly negative effects on the substantial minority of men (estimated at 25 to 30 percent of the male population) who are already predisposed to sexual violence and sexual abuse (Briere and Runtz 1989; Russell 1988).

The Indecent Displays Act of 1981 was passed in the wake of the Williams Committee Report and regulates the display of pornography in public places. It was not thought necessary then by politicians to define indecency, since the only concern was with how material was displayed, and not with what was sold or how it was used or the harm experienced by women and children as a result of its use.

In addition, the legislation was drafted to be impossible to implement and enforce, and is therefore unenforceable. An item judged obscene in one area can still sell legally in any other part of the country; it must be successfully prosecuted over and over again. Currently, it is the case that the Crown Prosecution Service will not prosecute adult pornography "on the grounds that there is no reasonable prospect of conviction" (Edwards 1992, 41).

In the UK, obscenity legislation has also been used to censor art and literature and to prosecute gay and lesbian material which is not pornography (Itzin 1992). It has, by contrast, been unable to deal with the increased production and circulation of increasingly sadistic pornography. Moreover, obscenity law is totally unable to deal with the technological ability of the pornography industry to "trade" across national boundaries through satellite broadcasting and computer networks.

Conflict Between UK and EU Legislation

Computer-generated pornography is one example of the technological expansion of the pornography industry which has been resistant to regulation through obscenity law. In the UK, much of the computer pornography is from North America, Scandinavia, Germany, and the Far East. According to Merchant (1994), everything available in other types of pornography, such as books and videos, is placed on computer disk: "In addition to the usual pornographic poses, I've seen graphic close-ups of apparent rape, torture and murder." With the exception of child pornography, it is not a criminal offense to possess such material, but it is to supply it or intend to supply it (Squires 1993, 6).

The Police Federation, in its evidence to the Home Affairs Committee on Computer Pornography, regarded it as a "major concern that children and young people have access to these systems" (1993, 3). They made a number of recommendations to strengthen the existing obscenity legislation, which included extending the categories of actionable materials to include computer data, treating acquisition of obscene material via computer as "importation of obscene material," and promoting more substantial penalties in the form of fines and prison sentences. They also recommended increased international cooperation but regarded the scope for cooperation to be limited because of variations in legislation internationally and, in particular, the liberal laws relating to pornography in Europe. Lastly, detection is a problem, particularly where material is transmitted over telephone lines into the UK from abroad.

Satellite broadcasting of pornography into the UK from Europe is another example of technology challenging the enforceability of obscenity legislation in the UK. This situation also demonstrates the ways in which UK obscenity legislation conflicts with European Community legislation. This problem has focused on the broadcasts from the Netherlands and a company called Red Hot Dutch that promotes sexually explicit material, categorized as "hard core" pornography. Under Section 153 of the 1990 Broadcasting Act, the

Broadcasting Standards Council (BSC) is required to monitor and to report to the Secretary of State on television programs which are transmitted from outside the UK, but which are capable of being received within the country. The BSC found that Red Hot Dutch broadcast films that promoted an association between aggression and sex. The Broadcasting Council, moreover, declared that women are "frequently shown in degrading and humiliating circumstances" (Broadcasting Standards Council 1993, 52–54). The BSC reported in November 1992 to the Secretary of State that, under Section 162 of the Broadcasting Act 1990, Red Hot Dutch would be liable to prosecution under the Obscene Publications Act of 1959.

In 1993, the UK government took action under this legislation to proscribe the satellite broadcasts by Red Hot Dutch, with the effect that anyone supplying equipment or advertising to the channel would be committing a criminal offense. Following the proscription, Red Hot Dutch ceased broadcasts and stated its intention to appeal to the European Court on grounds that the UK "ban" was in breach of EU law, and specifically in violation of a 1989 EC Directive on Broadcasting (89/552/EEC; OJ L 298/23, 17 October 1989). The Directive states that if a broadcast would not offend against the law of the originating Member State, then it cannot be subject to secondary controls in the receiving Member State. At this writing, the BSC was unaware of any further action having been taken by Red Hot Dutch.

In the meantime, Coleman and McMurtrie have outlined two ways in which the UK might end the satellite broadcasting of pornography "without offending against the terms of the 1989 Directive" (1993, 10). One of these would be to take advantage of the complicated procedures laid down in the Directive itself which would permit Member States to ban programs which violate Article 22 of the Directive. This Article states that "Member States shall ensure that broadcasts do not contain any incitement to hatred on grounds of race, sex, religion, or nationality." The other alternative would be to use Article 56 of the EEC Treaty, which asserts that the implementation of Treaty articles "shall not prejudice the applicability of provisions laid down by law ... providing for special treatment of foreign nationals on grounds of public policy, public security or public health." Using Article 56 could make it a criminal offense to promote Red Hot Dutch "by supplying equipment relative to the proscribed service; or by advertising on the channel; or by publishing transmission times and/or details of the programs" (Section 1768 of the 1990 Act).

Furthermore, Article 7 of the European Convention on Trans-frontier Broadcasting states that "all items of programme services ... shall respect the dignity of the human being and the fundamental rights of others." In particular, programs shall not "be indecent, or in particular, contain pornography" nor shall they "give undue prominence to violence or be likely to incite racial hatred."

Whatever the eventual outcome of the Red Hot Dutch case, it is clear from the UK experience of trying to deal with the national and international trade in pornography (in both its published and technological forms) that obscenity legislation is both inadequate and inappropriate in dealing with pornography.

United Nations Conventions as a Human Rights Framework

There are, however, more appropriate alternatives within which to conceptualize the harm of pornography and to construct harm-based legislation. One of these is to use United Nations conventions as a basis for legislating against pornography on the grounds of human rights violations. A number of United Nations instruments are relevant to the harm of pornography. Moreover, they constitute a clear benchmark which the European Court of Justice is expected to accept as binding within the field of Community law.

The *Universal Declaration of Human Rights* includes "rights to life, liberty and security of person" (Article 3), "to freedom of movement" (Article 13), "not to be held in slavery or servitude" (Article 4), and "not to be subjected to torture or degrading treatment" (Article 5). It states that:

> everyone is entitled to all the rights and freedoms set forth in this Declaration, without distinction of any kind such as race, color, sex, language, religion, political or other opinion, national or social origins, property, birth or other status.

All of these fundamental human rights are denied to or limited for women as a result of pornography. The *Universal Declaration of Human Rights* is only a declaration, but it is supported by the UN Charter which all Member States swear to uphold, and by a succession of covenants and conventions, and by UN agencies. The *European Convention on Human Rights* asserts that "no one shall be subjected to torture or to inhuman or degrading treatment or punishment" (Article 3) or "be held in slavery" (Article 4). The

Convention affirms "the right to freedom from discrimination on any ground including sex" (Article 14). Practices which violate this Convention are actionable under Community law.

The *International Covenant on Civil and Political Rights* (signed by all Member States) specifies that:

> all persons are equal before the law and entitled without any discrimination to the equal protection of the law. In this respect the law should prohibit any discrimination and guarantee to all persons equal and effective protection against discrimination on any grounds such as race, color, sex, language, religion, political or other opinion, national or social origin, property, birth or other status (Article 26).

The *Convention Against Torture and Other Cruel, Inhuman or Degrading Treatment or Punishment* (CAT) defines torture as "any act by which severe pain or suffering, whether physical or mental, is intentionally inflicted on a person," or "coercion based on discrimination of any kind."

The *Convention on the Elimination of All Forms of Discrimination Against Women* (CEDAW), a major human rights instrument adopted by the UN General Assembly on 18 December 1979, includes an Article (6) which calls for the suppression of all forms of traffic or trade in women and girls and of the exploitation of prostitution. CEDAW asserts that women have rights as individuals and as a social group, and thus could support the use of class actions (Ashworth 1993). In 1991, CEDAW adopted a General Resolution (18) on *Violence Against Women* in preparation for the 1993 World Conference on Human Rights, and a *Draft Declaration on Violence Against Woman* was drawn up for discussion at the 1992 Commission on the Status of Women. This affirms that "violence against women violates the enjoyment of women of human rights and fundamental freedoms" and recognizes that "violence is a manifestation of historically unequal power relations between men and women, which have led to domination over and discrimination against women by men." Article 1 defines violence against women as "gender-based violence that results in or is likely to result in physical, sexual or psychological harm or suffering to women."

The Third European Ministerial Conference on Equality Between Women and Men in 1993 considered strategies for the elimination of violence against women in society, which focused on the role of the media and produced a "Declaration on Policies for Combating Violence Against Women in a Democratic Europe," which in turn noted "the emergence of European networks for traffic in women." This declaration stressed in particular "the responsibility of the media with regard to the production, reproduction and distribution of violent, brutal or pornographic products" (Council of Europe 1993).

The above-noted instruments/statements are clearly important and pertinent to pornography in so far as they acknowledge gendered power relations and conceptualize gender-based violence and abuse as human rights violations. But, it must be recognized that these instruments have not achieved the status of statute, nor have they been articulated in the form of law that can be used to take action on behalf of women who have been victimized by and through prostitution or trafficking in pornography. Having had no explicit effect on the laws of individual Member States, their function and value has thus far been only symbolic.

And yet, as a symbolic framework, these instruments are not insignificant. In addition to their human rights potential, they also create a context within the European Union in which to develop a concept of women's citizenship and a recognition that violence and abuse against women in whatever form denies to women an opportunity to exercise their full citizenship (see Hanmer, Chapter 9). Within this symbolic framework there is an opportunity to develop a harm-based equality approach to legislation against pornography.

Equality Legislation

In the UK, there are precedents in existing equality legislation for legislating against the harms of pornography. The Sex Discrimination Acts of 1975 and 1986 make it unlawful to discriminate either directly or indirectly on the grounds of sex and, in particular, for any person to treat a woman less favorably than a man. The Equal Pay Act of 1970 stipulates equal treatment with respect to pay, contract, and conditions of employment for women and men who are doing the same or broadly similar work. There is also race relations legislation. The Race Relations Act of 1976 makes it unlawful to discriminate in employment on grounds of color, race, nationality, or ethnic or national origins. These are civil laws. However, incitement to racial hatred was made a criminal offense in the Race Relations Act of 1965, and this offense was transferred to the Public Order Act in 1986. This prohibits the use of "threatening, abusive or insulting" words or behavior and the publication, distribution, display, or possession of any materials which are "threatening, abusive, insulting" and "likely to incite racial hatred." It is not necessary to prove intent: "restrictions on racist speech have been accepted in terms of a general tendency or likelihood" (Easton 1994, 171).

There have been problems of enforcement with the incitement to racial hatred legislation. As with the Obscene Publications Act, prosecutions can be brought only with the consent of the Attorney General and the agreement of the Crown Prosecution Service. This is rarely forthcoming. Experts in race law believe, however, that incitement law could be an effective instrument if there were a "political will to make it so" (Bindman 1992, 262). They also believe that "even if the number of prosecutions is low, the existence of the law is important in demonstrating a public rejection of racism and marking the boundaries of acceptable speech" (Easton 1994, 169).

Freedom of speech has not been an unqualified human right, and there have been limits imposed on freedom of expression in the UK when it has contributed to "identifiable harm," as in the case of race hatred because of the acknowledged harm it does to Blacks and Jews. Although restraints on racist speech have been accepted in terms of "a general tendency or likelihood" of harm, "a much higher standard of proof has been required when assessing the harms of pornography" (Easton 1994, 170). Arguably, the harms related to pornography have been even more thoroughly evidenced than the harms resulting from racist speech. The case for legislation against incitement to sexual hatred and violence through pornography must therefore be as compelling as the case for legislation against incitement to racial hatred.

Harm-Based Equality Approach to Legislating Against Pornography Without Censorship

In the UK, there are currently proposals to use equality law as a basis for legislating against pornography based on the evidence of harm. One form of such harm-based legislation would be a civil law, a form of *sex discrimination/victim compensation legislation* that would enable people who could prove they were victims of pornography-related harm to take action against the manufacturers and distributors of pornography. This civil law could operate together with a criminal law against *incitement to sexual hatred and violence through pornography* based on the Race Relations Act of 1976 (Public Order Act 1986). The identifiable harm associated with the use of pornography would form the basis for legislating against incitement to sexual hatred and violence through pornography using the Race Relations model. Both forms of legislation would include a legal definition of pornography borrowed from the Civil Rights Ordinance drafted by Catharine A. MacKinnon and Andrea Dworkin (1988).

This definition of pornography contains two parts. First, it is defined as that which is graphic and sexually explicit and subordinates women. It must contain all three of these characteristics. Second, it must also include one or more specific conditions of harm in the form of sexual objectification or sexual violence. Specifically, this means women presented

1. dehumanized as sexual objects, things, or commodities, and/or
2. as sexual objects who enjoy humiliation or pain, and/or
3. as sexual objects experiencing sexual pleasure in rape, incest, or other sexual assault, and/or
4. as sexual objects tied up or cut up or mutilated or bruised or physically hurt, and/or
5. in postures or positions of sexual submission, servility, or display, and/or
6. being penetrated by objects or animals, and/or
7. in scenarios of degradation, humiliation, injury, torture, shown as filthy or inferior, bleeding, bruised, or hurt in a context that makes these conditions sexual, and/or
8. with women's body parts exhibited—including but not limited to vaginas, breasts or buttocks, and anuses—such that women are reduced to those parts.

Although this definition of pornography has been based on the sexualized subordination of women and eroticized violence against women, it has been drafted to include the use of men and children in the place of women. In this legal definition, pornography does not include sexually explicit material premised on equality or sex education materials. This is a very narrow definition which would target only sexually explicit material that is violent and subordinating and shown to be harmful.

The harm-based approach to legislating against pornography without censorship now has the formal support of hundreds of women's organizations in the UK. The National Alliance of Women's Organizations (NAWO), representing over two hundred women's organizations, has unanimously adopted a policy to "support legislation to enable people who can prove they are victims of pornography-related harm to take civil action against the manufacturers and distributors of pornography." This approach has the advantage of providing a way of legislating against pornography without censorship. There are also precedents to this approach in Belgian law; there, incitement to sexual exploitation against children and adults is illegal. A civil law would not ban the publication of pornography, and it would give no power to the state to censor. The law against incitement to racial hatred is not regarded by most Blacks and Jews as censorship, but as a guarantee of a measure of freedom from violence and discrimination.

Conclusion

There are certain freedoms that people have agreed to forgo because of the damage and harm they do to others. These include the freedom to steal, to assault, to rape, to murder, and in the UK to incite racial hatred and race discrimination, and to discriminate in employment on the grounds of race or sex. The freedom to incite sexual hatred, sexual violence, and sex discrimination through pornography is, arguably, another freedom people should agree to forgo in order to ensure and safeguard the civil liberties and human rights of women.

Adoption of a civil approach to pornography would enhance women's chances for greater freedom and safety from personal harm. The right of women to be free of the misrepresentation and mistreatment by pornography is arguably a fundamental human right with the potential for being addressed as such in European law.

6

Sexual Trafficking of Women in Europe

A Human Rights Crisis for the European Union

Dorchen Leidholdt

The massive and escalating sexual trafficking of women into and throughout Europe has created a human rights crisis of such immense proportions that the European Community has finally been forced to reckon with it, however reluctantly. In this chapter, I will discuss the nature and dimensions of the European sex trade in women, Europe's efforts to address it, and the reasons that Europe has been unable to arrive at effective strategies.

Dimensions of the Problem

What is sexual trafficking in women and how prevalent is it in Europe? Sexual trafficking in women is the movement of girls and women for purposes of sexual exploitation, usually from developing countries in Asia, Latin America, and Africa into the sex industry of developed countries. Sexual trafficking in women also encompasses the movement of girls and women from Eastern Europe and the former Soviet Union into Western Europe's brothels and sex businesses, as well as the movement of girls and women from Europe's rural areas into its industrial centers. From this angle, it is apparent that much of what is thought of as generic prostitution is in fact sexual trafficking (de Dios 1993).

One of the defining characteristics of sexual trafficking is that it removes girls and women from a world in which they have at least a semblance of a support system into a situation in which they are isolated from family, friends, and sources of help. Girls and women who are sexually trafficked are thrust into a situation in which communication with others is difficult. They often have a different dialect and frame of reference from those in the "host" country or, worse, do not speak that country's language.

Girls and women who are trafficked in for sex are put in situations of extreme dependence and sometimes imprisonment. They are, for example, required to pay their transportation costs to the "host" country at several times the real price. Once there, they have no place to stay, no money for housing, and they are beholden to those who provide shelter. Their means of returning to their homeland—their tickets and passports—are usually confiscated from them by their traffickers. They often are in a country illegally and, thus, are unable to go to the authorities for help (ICPO-INTERPOL 1988).

Finally, girls and women who are trafficked in are put into environments in which people of their racial or ethnic group are considered inferior and are thus subjected to additional discrimination. Not only do these girls and women have vastly less social and economic power than others in the unfamiliar world in which they find themselves, but their purpose in being there is to provide sexual gratification to members of the dominant gender of the dominant country by submitting to these men's racist and sexist stereotypes and fantasies. In other words, sexual trafficking puts already extremely vulnerable girls and women into the most powerless and dependent situation imaginable.

European immigration laws and policies reflecting anti-foreigner and racist sentiments intensify the dependence of women and girls from developing countries on traffickers and sex industry pimps. For example, the immigration laws in effect in the United Kingdom since 1949 greatly restrict the ability of immigrant women to seek out and hold ordinary jobs. In Switzerland, immigrant women working as dancers are permitted three-month contracts which can be renewed, at most, three times.[1] The Schengen Accord, signed in January 1985 among France, Germany, Italy, Portugal, and Spain, requires carriers to return any passenger suspected of being a criminal, terrorist, or undocumented worker. Philippine activist Aurora Javate de Dios points to the inevitable consequences of such restrictions:

---

1. In July 1994, the Swiss government announced a value-added tax that would apply to "sales" by prostitutes beginning in 1995. Customers would be supplied with itemized receipts showing the 6 percent tax.

These conditions make Asian women powerless and vulnerable to traffickers, fake marriage bureaus, and other shady intermediaries such as underworld syndicates like the Yakuza, Mafia, Triad, and others which have traditionally controlled migrant labor and entertainment industries ... the pressure to go underground will increase as will the dependence of women of color on European men who are not subject to these restrictions (1993, 7–8).

Against the powerlessness and dependence of the women who are trafficked, one must measure the power and ruthlessness of the economic interests that control the global sex industry.[2] They include organized crime syndicates, pimp networks, and brothel and sex shop owners, in alliance with legitimate businesses—hotel chains, travel agencies, employment agencies, airlines, and too often, government officials (ICPO-Interpol 1988, 24–27). To these traffickers, the women and girls they control are either invisible or are mere commodities that must be treated in ways that can generate the greatest profit possible.[3]

The traffic in women in Europe is often the direct result of European sex tourism. Such tourism generally involves white male travelers from primarily Germany, Holland, Belgium, Switzerland, and Scandinavia who take sex vacations to cities, towns, and resorts in Asia, Latin America, and Africa for the purpose of prostitution with local women and children (Tice 1992, 38).[4] The sex tourism industry that procures local women and girls as prostitutes and sex entertainers for moneyed European tourists works in association with the sex trafficking syndicates that then export these girls and women to Europe.

Why girls and women are susceptible to sex tour operators and sex traffickers is hardly a mystery. The vast majority are very poor. Most are supporting their families, which too often are willing to sacrifice their daughters for a better standard of living. Usually, the

2. For accounts of the methods and identities of traffickers as well as the conditions of their victims, see Chan (1993, 7); Gladwell and Stassen-Berger (1993, A10); Gambardello (1993); Kleinfield (1995, B1); and Praden (undated).

3. For information about the economic interests behind the international sex industry, see Leonora C. Angeles and the Philippine Organizing Team (1993).

4. Tice cites a Pacific News Service report (18 March 1991) that estimates that Thai prostitutes cater to an estimated 600,000 tourists, flown in by tour companies in the United States, Europe, Japan, and Australia. For more information on sex tourism, see Albertina Emelda, "Tourism as a Method of Exploitation for Prostitution both Nationally and Internationally" (1988), and Kim Hae Won, "The Realities of Kisaeng Tourism in Cheju Island" (1988).

girls and women have been socialized into an ethos of female servitude and self-sacrifice.

These girls and women may also be ambitious and adventurous. They may regard work as a dancer or hostess as the only way out of poverty or grueling manual labor and factory work. The agencies that procure them lie about what will actually be required once they reach their destination—unwanted sex with stranger after stranger, a concentration-camp existence in which every movement is monitored, rape and battering at the hands of customers and pimps, venereal disease, and the omnipresent threat of AIDS. In addition, the women and girls are under tremendous economic pressure as they try both to pay off their debts to their traffickers and to send money home to their families. The physical consequences of prostitution are innumerable and include infertility from repeated bouts of venereal disease, drug addiction, diseases like hepatitis B that accompany drug addiction, and death from AIDS (Maurer 1991). The psychological consequences include post-traumatic stress disorder and the destruction of the woman's sexuality and personality (Hoigard and Finstad 1992, 65–66).

The dimensions of the European sex trade in women and girls are enormous. In the Netherlands in 1991, approximately 60 percent of the 20,000 prostitutes were foreigners (Männson 1992, 2–3). Amsterdam's sex industry exploits an estimated 7,000 women and girls from the Dominican Republic alone (French 1992). Conservative estimates show that 12,000 Philippine women were living illegally in Germany in 1988, the vast majority in prostitution. This is an increase of 30 percent since 1984 (Lipka and Niesner 1988). When these figures are combined with corresponding data from other Western European countries, it becomes evident that as many as 100,000 women in Europe are existing in conditions of sexual exploitation, most trafficked from non-European countries (Männson 1992).

As for the statistics on European sex tourism, in 1988, 53,000 Swiss tourists visited Kenya, the site of a growing sex tourism industry; that same year 75,300 Swiss tourists went to Thailand, two-thirds of whom were male (Maurer 1991). In the Philippines, former United States military bases have been converted into sex tourism centers for primarily German, Swiss, and Australian sex tourists (Coalition Against Trafficking in Women 1993). Sex tours into Asia were especially popular among Norwegian sex tourists until Norwegian feminists began to give them send-offs at the airports.[5]

The geographic origins of the women and girls trafficked into Europe has shifted over the past three decades as the global sex industry has made inroads into new parts of the world. During the 1970s, the women trafficked into the brothels of Europe were primarily from East Asia, especially Thailand and the Philippines. The roots of this wave of trafficking were the organized prostitution around United States military bases in Vietnam and the Clark and Subic air bases in the Philippines.[6] The 1980s witnessed an influx of women and girls trafficked into Europe's brothels from Latin America and the Caribbean, especially the Dominican Republic, Brazil, and Colombia, but also Ecuador and Chile.[7]

5. The protests were organized by the Women's Front of Norway, representatives of which presented information about them at "Global Trafficking in Women," a conference organized by Women Against Pornography and held in New York City 22–23 October 1988. Subsequently, the protesters were sued for libel by Scan Thai Traveller Club, one of the tourist agencies they targeted. The court ruled in favor of the Women's Front, requiring Scan Thai to pay half the cost of the women's legal fees, and held that the organization's depiction of Scan Thai as fostering racial and sexual oppression was accurate: "Generally one must see prostitution as a form of exploitation of women and as oppression of women. When this oppression of women takes place in the Third World and is kept up by mass tourism from Western industrial countries, an element of racial discrimination is undoubtedly added to the sexism. ... The court concludes that these terms [the Women's Front's characterization of Scan Thai as "racist" and "sexist"] must be seen as having sufficient basis in the actual facts." Report from Nina Kristen, Chairwoman, Women's Front of Norway, 2 September 1988.

European sex tour agencies are often blatant about the type of vacation they are offering. The brochure of Germany's Rosie Travel states: "You can book a trip to Thailand with erotic pleasures included in the price" and Norway's Scan Thai Traveller publishes a guidebook that purports to offer its customers "a pep talk" replete with such encouragements as "Women in Bangkok you must pay for—for one night, for one week, or for your whole life. In return, they wish to give you a lot of care and sex."

6. Jill Gay writes, "the boom in Southeast Asian prostitution started with the U.S. presence in Vietnam. There were 20,000 prostitutes in Thailand in 1957; by 1964, after the United States established seven bases in the country, that number had skyrocketed to 400,000" (1985). See also Virginia A. Miralao, Cellia O. Carlos, and Aida Fulleros Santos (1990).

7. This information was obtained at the Conference on Trafficking in Latin American and Caribbean Women, 7–11 March 1993, Caracas, Venezuela. Materials on the commercial sexual exploitation of Latin American women can be obtained by writing the Coalition Against Trafficking in Women, Latin America. Urb. Montalban Res. Uslar E-2, Apto. 12, Final Calle 12 c/2d Avenida, Caracas 1021 Venezuela.

The most recent wave of sexual trafficking involves women trans-
ported into Europe from the former Soviet Union and into Western
Europe from Eastern Europe (Simons 1993). The reason for the
huge increase of sexual trafficking in Eastern European women and
girls is twofold. The dissolution of the Soviet state and the destruction of the Communist system has brought economic devastation
for many women. For example, in Russia, in 1991, women earned
75 percent as much as men, according to the Center for Gender
Studies in Moscow; in 1994, that figure dropped to 40 percent.
Unemployment for women in Russia is now three times higher than
it is for men. What social supports remain for Russian women are
rapidly being dismantled by the government; for example, the Moscow City Council recently proposed to close one-third of the city's
day care centers (Rimmel 1993, 9).

The second factor is the movement of organized crime syndicates into the vacuum left by the Soviet state, along with the green
light that the government has given to small-time pimps and profi-
teers (Morris 1993; Waxman 1993). Pornographic tabloids are
omnipresent. Russian women are subjected to unchecked sexual
harassment in the workplace, and mail-order bride businesses have
become the latest get-rich-quick scheme, exporting catalogues filled
with photos of bikini-clad women who were once doctors and engi-
neers (Rimmel 1993).

In the summer of 1993, during the World Conference on Human
Rights, my colleagues and I traveled to Budapest and found a city
whose center has been taken over by the sex industry. Advertising
for scantily clad blonde "international" prostitutes was everywhere.
Staid Vienna is also teeming with brothels filled with Eastern European and Turkish women,[8] and in Istanbul, Romanian women are
prostituted in growing numbers (Cowell 1993, 2).

The relation between Western Europe's prostituting of native-
born women and its trafficking in women from other countries is
significant and troubling. It is clear that those European countries
with the most established and legitimate prostitution systems also
have the greatest incidence of trafficking of women from poor countries. Germany and the Netherlands have legalized prostitution and

---

8. The *Haleo Wien Guide Book* (June 1993), available at the reception desks of
hotels throughout Vienna, contained five pages devoted to "escort services," strip
shows, and brothels.

legalized brothels, and they hold the largest population in Europe of women who have been trafficked (Brussa 1991; Männson 1992). What has evolved is a two-tier system of prostitution. The white German and Dutch-born prostitutes work in relatively luxurious government-approved brothels where customers are often required to use condoms. In September 1992 I spent several hours in a legal brothel in Frankfurt and talked at length with the women there. They were depressed and hopeless in spite of their opulent surroundings. Their plight, however, paled next to that of their Asian and Latin sisters working in nearby illegal brothels, servicing three or four times as many customers precisely because they did not or could not require their customers to wear condoms.

Organized and accepted prostitution within the borders of a developed country paves the way for organized trafficking of women from developing countries. It also appears that, as women in developed countries gain increasing social power and diminished vulnerability to sexual exploitation, the response of their male compatriots who want sexually subordinated women is either to join the ranks of the sex tourist or to patronize immigrant prostituted women. In this respect, the social and economic gains of so-called "First World" women has come at a terrible cost to many of our "Third World" sisters. Moreover, all women pay a price when the culture of prostitution permeates a society and women and girls are valued only as sexual merchandise (Saylan 1991).

An additional result of sexual trafficking in women in Europe is that Asian, African, and Latin women living or traveling in its countries are stigmatized as prostitutes. A Thai feminist activist told me in Frankfurt that she could not have her name listed in the telephone directory because she received calls from "johns" all night long. They assumed that because she was Thai, she must be a prostitute. This stereotyping is also inflicted on European women who travel from sending to receiving countries. Leaving Bucharest for Istanbul, a young Romanian woman, studying at an American university, told me of her fear that she would be stigmatized as a prostitute due to the heavy sex trafficking of Romanian women and girls into the brothels of Turkey. Recent reports on the situation of women in Russia—especially the revelation that women workers are now being openly recruited on the basis of their perceived sexual attractiveness to their employers (*New York Times*, 17 April 1994, 1)—demonstrate that the entire female population of a country can be defined and brought down by the sex industry.

Efforts to Address the Sex Trade

Although the issues of trafficking in women and prostitution have surfaced repeatedly in European legislative bodies and criminal justice agencies, little action has been taken. Nonetheless, some valuable statements of principle have been made. In 1958, for example, the Consultative Assembly of the Council of Europe unanimously adopted a resolution calling for the speedy ratification of the 1949 Convention for the Suppression of the Traffic in Persons and of the Exploitation of the Prostitution of Others.[9] In this resolution, the Consultative Assembly echoed the 1949 Convention's assertion that prostitution and sexual trafficking "are incompatible with the dignity and worth of the human person."[10] Although the Council of Europe is separate from the European Union, all EU Member States belong to the Council of Europe and purport to embrace its positions.

More recently, in June 1986, the European Parliament passed a resolution specifically addressing the contemporary industrialized sex trade in Europe. The Resolution on Violence Against Women urged Member States "to adopt a declaration on Community measures to combat trafficking in women, which focus primarily on preventative schemes to provide women (and thus their families) with alternative income opportunities and include the prosecution of those who traffic in women (OJ C 176/80, 11 June 1986)." It also calls on Member States "to ban all establishments catering to sex tourism, and to make all forms of sex tourism and the advertising thereof illegal" (OJ C 176/81, 11 June 1986). In particular, the Resolution targeted the customers, an extraordinary development, by calling attention to the "hypocrisy of those societies which condemn and penalize prostitutes, while their 'clients,' who are ultimately responsible for the prevalence of this phenomenon, have neither slur, nor stigma, nor prosecution to fear (OJ C 176/81, 11 June 1986)." The Resolution urged Member States to decriminalize prostitution and to prevent the prostitution of young women

9. The Council of Europe should not be confused with the European Commission or Council of Ministers. The Council of Europe is separate from the European Union and is distinguished by its promotion of a human rights agenda. The European Union, by contrast, retains an economic focus.

10. Consultative Assembly of the Council of Europe, Tenth Ordinary Session, Recommendation 161 (1958).

and facilitate their reintegration into society. To this end, it called
for the provision of drug rehabilitation and job training for prostituted women and girls. It concluded by imploring Member States
to prepare young people for adult relationships "based on the fundamental acceptance of the equality of all individuals, with a view
to creating a feeling of mutual responsibility and respect" (OJ C
176/82, 11 June 1986).

The understanding of prostitution and sex trafficking reflected in
this Resolution was even further developed in the European Parliament's 1989 Resolution on the Exploitation of Prostitution and the
Traffic in Human Beings (OJ C 120/352, 14 April 1989). This
statement recognized that "the practice of prostitution involves the
violation of certain fundamental human rights and freedoms, especially the rights to privacy, liberty and the integrity of the human
person," and it urged the development of "a genuine common policy adopted by all the Member States in order to combat prostitution and eliminate the traffic in persons." This 1989 Resolution
called for fundamental change "in the attitudes of men, women, the
media, and social institutions in general, which will make it possible to discard the stereotype of women as a mere object of sexual
pleasure." The Resolution also suggested specific legal remedies,
including increased penalties against pimps, procurers, and traffickers, assistance to victims of trafficking, especially in prosecuting
their exploiters, and the creation of a special division of the police
force, staffed by women, to receive victim's complaints and provide
them with social services.

It appeared that the European Parliament was on the verge of
spearheading fundamental and welcome changes in both policy
and laws related to prostitution and sexual trafficking. Certainly,
these resolutions reveal a sophisticated and feminist understanding of the problem and well-reasoned strategies for addressing it.
Some commentators have suggested that the European Parliament has a more sophisticated understanding of sexual subordination and is unrestrained in promoting it because, in part, it lacks
the power to implement its more progressive agenda. It is not a
matter of coincidence that this EU institution has been at once the
most democratic and least powerful (see Elman's introduction and
Baer's chapter). Nonetheless, it would be wrong to dismiss the
positions taken by it as merely symbolic. The power of the European Parliament is growing, and this body is influential—its resolutions both reflect and reinforce the human rights agenda of
its membership.

Efforts to Maintain and Promote
Sexual Trafficking[11]

A very different understanding of prostitution and sexual trafficking, however, was emerging from more powerful EU institutions as well as within those countries in which the sex industry was most entrenched.[12] The argument that prostitution is a profession and as such grants EEC nationals free movement within Europe, explicitly rejected by the Dutch Crown in 1975, would later be accommodated by the European Court of Justice in 1982.

In the 1975 case the Dutch Crown affirmed a decision by the Ministry of Justice denying a Belgian woman a residence permit because she supported herself through prostitution. Hardly a victory for women's rights, the decisions of both the lower and the appellate courts dismissed out of hand the petitioner's argument that although she was in prostitution, she had come to the Netherlands not to work as a prostitute but because she was fleeing an abusive husband. The courts' assertion that prostitutes are "not of good moral conduct" reflects both their lack of understanding of the conditions that propel and keep women in prostitution and a double standard—after all prostitution was and is legal in the Netherlands. The only comfort feminists could draw from the Crown's decision was that, by accepting the Ministry of Justice's conclusion that "the profession of a prostitute cannot be considered as 'carrying out work' ...," the highest court of the Netherlands was refusing to legitimize prostitution, a position that put it at odds with the Dutch legislature.

A very different result was reached by the European Court of Justice in 1982 when two cases were joined before it. Both involved French women who were denied permission to reside in Belgium because each had a history of prostitution. The Court ruled that Articles 48 and 56 of the EEC "do not permit a member-State to expel a national of another member-State ... on the grounds of personal conduct" if there are not "genuine or effective measures intended to combat such conduct for local nationals" (*Adoui and Cornuaille v. Belgian State* Joined Cases 115 and 116/81 [1982] 3

---

11. R. Amy Elman brought to my attention the legal cases discussed in this section and was instrumental in the analysis of them.

12. *Re A Belgian Prostitute, The Queen of the Netherlands in Council*, [1976] 2 CMLR 527, 7 January 1975 at 530.

CMLR 631). Given the absence of anti-prostitution laws in Belgium, the Court held that nationals from other Member States have a right to reside in Belgium and carry out the same work as nationals from the host Member State.

One can hardly quarrel with the result of the decision. Member States that take no serious measures to eliminate prostitution but in fact profit from it by taxing the earnings of prostitutes should not be able to discriminate against prostitutes from other Member States by refusing them residence permits on public policy grounds. Nonetheless, this decision contributes to the legitimization of prostitution by regarding it as "personal conduct" and a "profession." At the same time, the decision facilitates the trafficking of EEC nationals to other Member States where prostitution is either legal or the prohibitions against it are neither "genuine" nor "effective."

The significance of this 1982 ruling appears to have escaped the attention of most EU commentators. However, a decade later, Swedish feminists cited the decision as indicative of the EU's indifference towards women (Kvinnofronten 1993, 26). Despite their vigorous opposition to Sweden's entrance into the Common Market, Swedish voters provided a slim majority favoring the EU, and the country entered an enlarged Union (of now fifteen members) in January of 1995.[13]

The analysis of prostitution implicit in the 1982 decision of the European Court of Justice was made explicit in a 1991 seminar I attended, entitled "Action Against Traffic in Women and Forced Prostitution." The meeting was sponsored by the Council of Europe's European Committee for Equality Between Women and Men, in conjunction with the Dutch government.

From the start of the seminar, it was apparent that the Dutch participants were running the meeting. The chair was Dutch and the vast majority of the officials espoused what became known as "the Dutch position." The gist of their presentations was as follows: "coerced prostitution" and "forced trafficking" are social problems that must be viewed as distinct and separate from the prostitution of women in their own countries and the "migration" of Third World women into First World sex centers. Whereas "coerced" prostitution and trafficking constitute a violation of human rights and human dignity, prostitution and related "migration" more generally are a function of individual choice, self-determination, sexual independence, and the natural and inevitable desire of workers to

---

13. Norway, by contrast, remained outside. See Hoskyns, note 12.

move into the most lucrative professions. In other words, the problem is not sexual trafficking per se, but certain abuses that take place when the industry is not adequately policed and regulated. The solution to the subordination of women in the sex industry is for women "sex workers" to organize "prostitutes' collectives" and thus become "empowered." Prostitution is "a job"; the relation between prostitute and customer is "a contract"; pimps and procurers were almost absent from the discussion.

The proponents of this pro-prostitution/pro-trafficking position strongly opposed the 1949 Convention, arguing that it failed to make an adequate distinction between "forced" and "free" prostitution. They explained that the Convention's prohibition of the business interests that organize and profit from prostitution, whether or not it is overtly coerced, represents an attack on "voluntary" prostitution. They did not regard the business networks—the brothels, sex shops, mail-order bride businesses, and trafficking cartels—as inherently coercive. What they argued for instead of the 1949 Convention is a Convention Against Forced Trafficking. Their preferred Convention would permit only those women who can prove in a court of law that they have been coerced by traffickers to take criminal action against their exploiters. Additionally, their Convention made no mention of pimping and procuring. It would leave pimps untouched, unless they resorted to overt forms of coercion in recruiting women. They also proposed a neo-regulatory scheme that would police the activities of the sex industry through consumer codes of conduct and "better business practices." For example, mail-order bride companies would adopt guidelines and regulations so that prospective clients would be screened before "marriages" take place.

What became clear at the seminar was that the sex industry has made tremendous economic and ideological inroads. Within Germany and the Netherlands in particular, there is a powerful pro-prostitution lobby. It includes many progressive activists who have made peace with the sex industry. These activists accept the sexual exploitation of women as a given, and invest their energy into helping women gain power within an industry that is fundamentally hostile to women's interests and functions as a vehicle for male domination. The enormous contradictions inherent in this position are hidden behind noisy invocations of "women's choice" and "women's empowerment." The specific outcome of the Council's Strasbourg meeting was the formation of a working group on "forced" prostitution and trafficking that has been paralyzed by an ideological impasse.

Conclusion

The possibility of breaking this deadlock has emerged from the development of an international Coalition Against Trafficking in Women, with strong regional organizations in Latin America and Asia. The Coalition has directly taken on the pro-prostitution lobby in Europe, identifying it as a sex industry front. The Coalition has repudiated any distinction between "forced" and "free" prostitution and trafficking as an effort to legitimize the sex trade in women. The Coalition's principal project—a proposed Convention Against Sexual Exploitation—has been endorsed by several influential European-based nongovernmental organizations, including the International Federation for Human Rights and the International Council of Women. It has also received strong support from UNESCO, the Belgian-French Community, and a group of European human rights jurists.

It is yet to be seen which path the European Union will take on the issue of sex trafficking and prostitution. Will it follow the lead of the European Parliament, with its Resolutions of 1986 and 1989; will it embrace the "Dutch position" promoted at the Council of Europe's Strasbourg seminar; or will it be frozen into inaction by the debate? Whatever course it takes will have profound implications, not only for the women of Europe, but for the women of the world.

7

REPRODUCTIVE TECHNOLOGIES IN GERMANY

An Issue for the European Union

Ute Winkler

This chapter provides a historical overview and critical appraisal of reproductive technologies with a focus on Germany. It notes that while Germany and other Member States have regulated these technologies, the absence of Union-wide regulations results in, among other problems, "reproductive tourism." This chapter seeks to enhance our understanding of this issue and calls for steps to be taken to end the technological exploitation and manipulation of women's reproductive capacities.

In 1978, the world witnessed a living, medical-technical miracle: reproductive medical doctors in England presented the first test-tube baby, the first successful lab experiment to unite maternal egg and paternal sperm. The public reaction was one of concern rather than delight. The women's movement was most vehement in its opposition to this development. They feared the realization of the patriarchal fantasy which suggests the eradication of women, if not completely, at least in matters of reproduction.[1] Liberating women from reproduction, promoting social emancipation and gender equality through medical technology, was less accepted in Germany than in many other countries.[2]

In the nearly two decades that followed the test-tube miracle, researchers have been engaged in what had previously been conceived

---

1. One need only consider the Euripidean tragedy, *Medea*. He exclaims: "It would have been better far for men / To have got their children in some other way, and women / Not to have existed. Then life would have been good" (*Euripides I* 1944, Lines 573–575).

2. One of the best-known representatives of the thesis that women must be liberated from childbearing is Shulamith Firestone (1971). See also Rowland (1987).

as utopian: egg and embryo donation, freezing and defrosting sperm, eggs and embryos, sex predetermination and chromosomal analysis, and genetic screening before embryo transfer. The once spectacular has become mundane. A multitude of reproductive technologies are currently in use and procedures like in vitro fertilization (IVF) have become increasingly popular.[3] The success rates of such treatments are, however, extremely small (approximately 5 percent); there are very serious side effects, risks, and long-term consequences for women, many of which remain unknown or are denied by doctors (see Klein 1989).

The qualitative assessment of embryos and fetuses through prenatal diagnosis has been less popular. In Germany, several medical techniques during pregnancy care are, nonetheless, utilized to this end. These techniques include ultra-sound, blood tests, amniocentesis, chorionic villi sampling, as well as the pre-implantation diagnoses.[4] This last technique entails the genetic checkup of the embryo before it is transferred into the uterus. Such methods demonstrate the close relationship between reproductive and genetic technologies.

The methods of reproductive technologies have gradually become an entrenched social norm with many serious biological, physical, psychological, and social consequences. These technologies change our attitudes towards procreation, sexuality, our bodies, fertility and infertility, health and illness, kinship and origin, genealogy, and even our attitude towards life and death. Reproductive technologies represent an assault on our morality, our logic, tradition, culture, and language. They represent rational-technical behavior in the field of procreation. These inventions mean control, expropriation,

---

3. In vitro, meaning in glass, is the opposite of in vivo, meaning in the living. In vitro fertilization (IVF) refers to fertilization that takes place outside the body (e.g., in a petri dish). IVF is a collective concept describing a complex medical procedure which consists of numerous, partial steps: (1) the stimulation of multiple ovulations through various hormonal inducements; (2) induced egg cell production shortly before ovulation; (3) actual test-tube fertilization and embryonic cultivation; (4) embryonic transfer (i.e., the process by which fertilized egg cells are placed within a uterus).

4. Chorionic villi sampling (CVS) refers to a procedure in which a small amount of chorion tissue surrounding the fetus is removed through the cervix between the eighth to fourteenth week of pregnancy. An analysis is then completed on the chromosomal and genetic status of the embryo including the determination of the sex. Amniocentesis is a prenatal diagnostic test done after the sixteenth week. It diagnoses certain "fetal abnormalities" (such as Down Syndrome and spina bifida) and is also used to determine the sex of the fetus. Both CVS and amniocentesis hold different risks which, among others, include miscarriages, hurting the baby, and diagnostic errors.

and the artificial production of life, as well as a qualitative valuation of human life and its destruction. Moreover, they mean more power for men, especially over women and their bodies. They mean less power for women, especially over their bodies and reproductive lives because women, not men, are the target group for the use of reproductive technologies. Also, men, not women, control the means of reproductive technologies.

The German Case

In Germany, and in the former Federal Republic in particular, there are two notable characteristics pertaining to reproductive technologies. First, the country has had the most restrictive regulations in the world for infertility treatments. Second, German reflections and discussions relating to these technologies are often of a critical nature. This critical assessment is essentially sustained by the women's movement, although other quarters remain vigilant in their opposition. Two massive conferences have been especially significant in providing a discerning appraisal of reproductive technologies. The first conference, "Women against reproductive technologies and genetic engineering," convened in Bonn in 1985. Two years later more than two thousand women attended a similar symposium in Frankfurt. Protests against reproductive technologies have come from the disability movement, religious groups, trade unions, and political parties as well.

By contrast, there has been almost no public debate in the former German Democratic Republic about the problems associated with reproductive treatments like IVF and prenatal diagnosis—both of which have been used. This relative lack of interest may be closely connected to the political system of the former GDR.

After unification in 1990, East Germans were consumed by different issues and politically explosive problems that they considered to be of greater relevance. These included high unemployment (particularly for women) and a radical transformation of an entire political, social, and cultural system of what was once the German Democratic Republic. Confronted with West German discourse, people in East Germany cared little about criticizing and regulating reproductive technologies. Indeed, such technologies (e.g., sterilization) were sometimes embraced to increase their chances for employment. East German women wished to promote themselves as reliable workers, uninterrupted by pregnancy and childcare concerns. The topic of reproductive technologies assumes a relatively marginal dimension despite some recent changes; for example, an East German women's journal (*Weibblick*) has published a special issue on genetic and reproductive technologies (September 1994). Lectures and other public events are also taking place.

In 1991, a newly unified Germany adopted the so-called Embryo Protection Law. It forbids egg donation, embryo donation, and surrogacy. The Embryo Protection Law is a criminal law, the violation of which is punishable by imprisonment (of up to five years) or a fine. To date, there have been no prosecutions for the medical professionals or women who have violated this law.

Not all reproductive technologies have been prohibited. The Embryo Protection Law does permit the transference of a woman's own embryos, three per IVF therapy cycle. This embryonic limit exists to reduce the risk of multiple pregnancies, especially the production of quadruplets or more. In addition, donor sperm, IVF, and artificial insemination are permitted.[5] Heterosexual couples are the primary users of these procedures and, with few exceptions, these treatments may not be used by those who are not married.

There is, at present, a debate concerning whether the latest treatments should also be forbidden. Micro-injections are under discussion. This procedure entails the injection of a single sperm cell into the egg cell. Through this technology virtually every man with fertility problems can still become a genetic father. Objecting to any further encroachments on their working conditions, the medical profession is strictly against any reforms. Although Germany has the most restrictive laws in the world, German medical doctors maintain their connections to international networks and research standards. Despite the Embryo Protection Law, they still participate in scientific research at the international level and create new treatments, many of which they test on women.

The legal regulation of reproductive technologies was never a major demand of the German women's movement. Nonetheless, debates persist about various legal approaches to these technologies. For example, together with the Green Party, feminists demanded abandonment of the Embryo Protection Law and, instead, enactment of a "women's protection law"; a demand which contained an

---

5. Artificial insemination by a husband's sperm (AIH) and by donor sperm (AID) is allowed, as are homolog IVF (both egg and sperm are from the couple) and heterolog IVF with donor sperm.

extensive ban on reproductive technologies.[6] Also, women have criticized the current law for separating the pregnant woman from the embryo, the legal implication being that women serve merely as a "fetal environment," a term used to describe pregnant women in the first draft of the law. In consequence, this law casts the embryo as a patient whose interests must be considered above those of the pregnant woman. The goal of this law was not to afford women protection from the existing risks associated with infertility treatments, but rather to regulate embryo production.

Although the 1991 law has curtailed extensive reproductive abuse, IVF was concomitantly legitimized as a major, "normal" treatment of infertility. No mention was made of the physical, psychological, and social side effects and risks associated with the use and further development of reproductive technologies.

The 1991 law created the impression that the state had imposed all necessary regulations and, therefore, news from other countries held limited significance for the Federal Republic. In Italy a sixty-year-old woman became a mother for the first time. Debate in France centered on the legal introduction of an age limit for biological motherhood. In England, virgin procreation and pre-implantation diagnosis was being discussed. In the Netherlands, lesbians can get a child through insemination or IVF. In Sweden, where lesbians are specifically prohibited from using artificial insemination, they often travel elsewhere in Europe for the procedure. Research with "artificial wombs" continues in Italy, and the cloning of embryos proceeds in the United States.

Reproductive Tourism and the European Union

It is well known that German women travel to different countries to access the reproductive possibilities that are not available to them within Germany. This is referred to as "reproductive tourism." For

6. This alliance is noteworthy. Feminist scholar and medical ethicist Jan Raymond states that too often "toxic reproductive chemicals are exempted from environmental consciousness." Environmental engineer H. Patricia Hynes asks: "As a wave of green lifestyle washes over industrial countries, making people conscious of not putting any unnecessary synthetic chemical substances on and into their body, why are women being advised to use synthetic hormones?" (in Raymond 1993, 133). Raymond suggests that women are "being exempted from the natural world as more and more bodily processes become subject to the medicalization of technological progress" (1993, 134).

example, when egg cell donation was outlawed in Germany, many women went to Austria. After procedures were legally forbidden there as well, clinics would then refer women to Budapest, Hungary. Little is now known about the extent to which the European Union supports this form of tourism or will make it more difficult for it to flourish. For example, it remains unclear whether advertisements are permitted to appear in German newspapers for procedures that are forbidden in the Federal Republic. What is certain is that laws could be changed to prevent this. More specifically, the European Union could adopt a common legal regulation concerning reproductive technologies and their numerous consequences. However, this has not been done.

It can be expected that the various laws of individual Member States will be made uniform in the area of reproductive medicine. That is, a short-term regulation can be expected in the near future. Just recently, France urged the EU to harmonize rules on artificial fertilization so as to discourage "medical tourism." However, experts assume that a liberal regulation will be implemented which will allow for a variety of procedures and will forbid virtually nothing. France's call for Union involvement is a case in point. Former French Health Minister Philippe Douste-Bluzy wished merely to limit artificial fertilization to infertile heterosexual couples of child-bearing age. Simone Veil, former French Social Affairs Minister, explained that "the Government wanted to prevent older women and those without stable partners from using artificial fertilization" (*New York Times*, 7 January 1994, 5). Restricting the use of these technologies to younger heterosexual "stable couples" is unlikely to stem the tide of reproductive tourism. In addition, a liberal regulation is likely to be of little consequence in the area of applied techniques (such as sterility therapies) and research.

Whatever action the EU adopts, the debates concerning abortion are likely to be reignited. Dutch political scientist Joyce Outshoorn notes that reproductive technologies "have touched off new debates on the beginning of human life, which may call abortion into question." Because several Member States prohibit abortion after viability, technological innovations may eventually expand restrictions on abortion. Outshoorn perceptively concludes that technological encroachments on reproduction have led to the "increased power of the medical professionals over human reproduction"—a development "probably more threatening to women's control over their own fertility than the anti-abortion groups" (1988, 218).

Abortion Politics

In Germany, the use of prenatal diagnostic methods is indirectly regulated through Bill 218 of the German abortion law. At present, an abortion is possible up until twelve weeks after conception.[7] First, however, the pregnant woman must undergo counseling specifically designed to dissuade her from terminating the pregnancy. Pregnant women are encouraged to consider the "high worth" of prenatal life. They are informed of the possibilities of financial support, should they choose to continue their pregnancy. Women often regard such anti-abortion efforts as "pressure counseling."

After German unification, a new abortion law was required. In the former German Democratic Republic, abortion was legal during the first three months of pregnancy. In the former Federal Republic of Germany, women had to meet specific social, medical or genetic criteria before they were legally permitted to have an abortion. According to the unification agreement, both laws had to be assimilated by the end of 1992. The result was the above-mentioned counseling model which was later declared unconstitutional through the Federal Constitutional Court. At present, a new regulation has not been issued. For the women of former East Germany, the constitutional readjustment entails a reduction of abortion possibilities and a loss of control over reproductive decisions. A vehement discussion ensued. Abortion was essentially cast as a woman's fundamental right: one which should be free and without governmental restriction and control.

During this time, however, little attention was given to the medical and technical developments pertaining to reproduction. Given the various prenatal diagnostic methods that were recently developed, the qualitative control of embryos was now possible. In particular, amniocentesis and chorionic villus sampling that result in abortions necessarily entailed an appraisal of the embryo/fetus. The principle of "worthy" and "unworthy" life has been enacted. Even in those instances in which a woman's particular reasons are very understandable, a decision to abort a fetus after amniocentesis is

7. Abortions are also permitted until twenty-two weeks after conception if the fetus can be shown to be suffering from a "non-removable" health defect that is otherwise non-treatable. This is what is meant by the so-called "eugenic" or "embryopathic" indication. A pre-implantation diagnostic is forbidden through the Embryo Protection Law.

always a eugenic decision. The standard of value for "worthy" or "unworthy" life is determined by medical science itself. Illness and genetic disposition are therapeutically judged and/or diagnosed inside the womb. Consequently, women are increasingly under the illusion that abnormal fetuses are a risk which can be identified and eliminated through medicine in general and reproductive technologies and genetic engineering in particular. Typically, reproductive technologies are justified as a means to avoid and/or reduce such risks. The fear women have of potential abnormalities is the chief reason why many undergo procedures such as amniocentesis. In utilizing reproductive technologies, women begin to suppose a certainty for perfection which does not exist. In the end, they are held responsible for the quality of the next generation. This is asking the impossible from women.

The German Past—Influencing the Present

Relative to other countries, Germany approaches reproductive and genetic technologies with both greater resistance and sensibility. The reason for this is closely connected with German history and more specifically the fascism of the Third Reich. Many Germans have had experience with direct, massive, state-led, and militarily enforced initiatives that controlled human reproduction. This tradition is, sometimes without interruption, part of today's practice and is legitimated through human genetic and reproductive medicine.

Reproductive technologies, especially those involving prenatal diagnosis, provide for a reexamination and continued discussion of German euthanasia and eugenic policies. The taboo that once cloaked this discussion is broken. The present standardization of human life does not take place violently, but through the popularization of scientific thinking. Science and medicine have seized the power to define life and change our biological and social reality. There is a similar trend toward the so-called "geneticization" of disability. Illness and disabilities are more often attributed to genetic as opposed to social causes. This approach is exemplified by prenatal genetic technologies. Moreover, reproductive technologies are credited with providing solutions to health problems.

Under fascism, the enforcement of rational, technical, eugenic, social, and misogynist procreation resulted from state control. The current approach to such procreation emanates less from the state than from the individual whose use of different infertility treatments (e.g., IVF and prenatal diagnosis) is apparently voluntary. Underscoring the voluntary aspects of such treatments is one of the greatest myths of reproductive medicine. Although infertility treatments have been used for less than twenty years in medical practice, evidence suggests that they are socially required. After all, women are often held individually responsible if they give birth to a disabled child. And, despite the many reasons for infertility, ranging from pollution to unsuitable contraception like the Dalkon Shield, women are similarly blamed. This same individualization of responsibility also occurs with regard to the use of reproductive technologies. Women are declared responsible when they use them and irresponsible when they do not.

Human procreation is never entirely natural. It is always the result of social and historical conditions. In our patriarchal society, women exercise relatively limited control over their lives and bodies. Reproductive technologies are founded upon patriarchal thinking which informs science and research. These technologies are legitimized by the language surrounding their use. It is a language that suggests a greater number of possibilities and freedom of choice for women. For example, women can either be infertile or have a test-tube baby; women can undergo amniocentesis or have a disabled child. The nearly unlimited offerings of reproductive medicine does not translate to greater freedom for women but rather greater (moral) pressure on them. Within this context, women are pressured to use nearly every form of reproductive assistance available to them. This pressure assumes the appearance of social agreement. Refusal to participate in medical-technical solutions to infertility or disability has become socially unacceptable.

Structural Inequalities

The structural inequities of reproductive technologies cannot be mitigated by extending their availability and making them accessible to all women. In Germany, where infertility treatments like IVF and prenatal diagnosis are paid for by the state through social health insurance, not every involuntarily childless woman or pregnant woman over thirty-five years of age uses the various technologies. While utilization of these technologies is, thus, not limited by financial considerations, mostly middle-class women use them.

Apparently these women have already accepted the new rational-technical approach to procreation.[8]

Reproductive technologies are not offered equally in all countries. More importantly, their uses vary depending on the population that is targeted. For example, treatments to enhance fertility (like IVF) are generally predominant among those populations that fear low birthrates within Europe, Australia, and the United States.[9] Reproductive technologies are not, however, limited to the promotion of fertility. They are also central to population policies designed to counter "over-production" particularly among women in Asia, Latin America, and Africa. The methods of reproductive science can be employed in different ways; for example, amniocentesis is not only used to identify "disabled" fetuses, but it is also used to determine the sex of the fetus. The abortion of female fetuses after amniocentesis is not uncommon. India is one of the best known examples of this; annually, tens of thousands of female fetuses are aborted because of their sex. In response, the Indian women's movement has launched massive protests that led to the illegalization of amniocentesis for the purpose of determining the sex of the fetus in several states (Gupta 1991).

The notion that female fertility, not male-dominated sexuality, is out of control serves as a justification for the development and use of anti-fertility technologies. These technologies include contraceptives like Depro-Provera, implants like Norplant and the increasingly popular anti-fertility vaccines.[10] Their use is directed against women as if their child-bearing capacities were a disease in need of

---

8. A class-specific use of reproductive technology is especially evident in the United States. Rates of infertility are highest among the lower social strata and yet the clientele for high-tech fertility procedures are largely from the middle and upper classes. At the same time, however, lower-income women (mostly non-white women) are being urged to reduce the number of children they have and are encouraged to make use of prenatal diagnostic methods (Lorber 1988).

9. However, the use of these technologies varies within Western countries. For example, poor white women and African-American women are the recipients of treatments to reduce their fertility in the United States. In Germany this is true, for example, for Turkish women immigrants. Moreover, contraceptives are given to disabled women, often without their informed consent, or they are even sterilized against their will. ·

10. Anti-fertility technologies refer to the new generation of contraceptives which are characterized by their long-term effectiveness. So, for example, Depro-Provera works for three months while implants can last for up to five years. At present, immunization procedures against pregnancy are being clinically tested. It is uncertain whether such technologies will lead to irreversible infertility. Still, many of the

treatment. Together with the medical establishment, policy experts labor under state control and within international organizations. They are engaged in the production of fertility in Western countries and the promotion of infertility in less industrialized nations.

Conclusion

Reproductive technologies have not been created to liberate women from the "social burdens" of procreation. Rather, the opposite seems to be true. Women are increasingly tied to their childbearing capacities. Now, with technology, women can give birth throughout their lives. Will some women be expected to utilize the technologies to this end while others are expected to be infertile? Reproductive technologies do not give more freedom to women because with them, women are losing their individual and social freedom. That is not to say, however, that such technologies do not offer help to some women in certain instances. After all, IVF can help "single" women to become genetic and biological mothers. In addition, prenatal diagnosis can diminish the fear women might otherwise have of giving birth to a child that might be disabled. These token instances do not, however, vitiate the assertion that reproductive technologies will never present *collective* freedom for women.

If we are to ensure a future in which life need not be dependent upon the logic of medical, technical, male-dominated science, we must oppose reproductive technologies. Medical-technical solutions cannot foster justice for women. Scientific solutions are ineffectual because science itself must change. Social and political solutions are necessary for such change. The European Union is certain to promote policy concerning reproductive technologies; feminism is the movement that must provide the context.

---

contraceptives that are now on the market and readily available have very serious side effects, leading to numerous health risks such as general malaise, long-lasting menstruations, disruptions of the menstrual cycle, and complete infertility. A further characteristic of these contraceptives is that they are being distributed almost exclusively to women in the so-called "Third World." Behind this lies the assumption that supposedly effective contraceptive techniques can stop rising populations in the countries throughout Asia, Africa, and South America. Through horror scenarios like "overpopulation" or "population explosion," it is being suggested that the earth will collapse unless strategic efforts are planned in the "right location" to reduce population growth, namely in the "Third World."

8

"AND NOBODY WAS ANY THE WISER"
Irish Abortion Rights and the European Union

Ailbhe Smyth

"And nobody was any the wiser"

Folklorist Anne O'Connor records that "infanticide as a way of getting rid of unwanted babies was more usually practiced [in Ireland] than abortion" and cites the following account by a woman informant:

> When a single girl found she was pregnant, she was so worried and could tell nobody, or get any help, she decided she would kill her child when born, and I have heard where such children were buried in fields. In some cases the guards came to investigate, but nothing much was ever found out about whether she buried her baby or not. In some cases her friends helped her to do away with her child secretly and nobody was any the wiser (O'Connor 1985).

Of course, this kind of thing doesn't happen any more in modern states. Or does it?

As 1993 became 1994, no fewer than *three* cases of infanticide were reported in the Irish media. These were the cases we heard about. How many more never made the headlines? How many cases of infanticide, from one year to another, are ignored, denied, disguised, recorded as "natural" infant death?

Infanticide is the extreme but strictly logical consequence, with suicide, of a social system in which women do not have control over their bodies, their sexuality, and reproduction. While abortion is rarely women's first (or even second) choice as a means of contraception (it is the means women are forced to "choose" when there is no choice), infanticide is indubitably the very rock-bottom of despair and the absolute deprivation of choice.

The question is—must be—what kind of "modern" society is this where women's needs are so desperate, and so far from being met, that they can have recourse to such extreme "solutions" to the "problem" of survival? To be sure, there is no one definition of "modernity," but however we define it, whatever indicators we use, infanticide is not among them. It is rather the tragic and disgraceful outcome—more frequent than we may realize—of the ferocious and barbaric oppression of women as human persons.

The "X" Case and the Right to Abortion in Ireland

The highly controversial and much publicized Irish abortion case of 1992 was again in the news in the summer of 1994. A forty-three year old man was sentenced to fourteen years imprisonment after pleading guilty to three charges of sexual offenses against the fourteen-year-old girl referred to as "X" in the court hearings on this landmark case. The case had come to public notice when the Irish Attorney General, acting on information from the Gardai (Irish police), obtained a court order preventing "X" from traveling to England for an abortion.

Although the Offenses Against the Persons Act (1861) already prohibited abortion, the right to life of the "unborn" had been formally guaranteed in the 8th Amendment to the Irish Constitution, voted by referendum in 1983. The text of this amendment (still in force) is as follows:

> The State acknowledges the right to life of the unborn and, with due regard to the equal right to life of the mother guarantees in its laws to respect, and as far as practicable, by its laws to defend and vindicate that right (Article 40.3.3).

Precisely *how* the State was to legislate for the supposedly "equal rights" of "unborn" and "mother" was not specified, no more than was the meaning of the phrase "as far as practicable." The only absolute certainty was that women would pay the price of this extraordinary amendment with their freedom, and even their lives. Women's status as citizens was gravely diminished by this amendment in that their constitutional rights of privacy, of association, of freedom of expression, and of movement were seriously curtailed. The "X" case proved to be the "nightmare scenario" predicted by all those who had opposed the insertion in the Constitution of this ambiguous, confused, and dangerous amendment.

The Attorney General's action in the "X" case provoked widespread outrage and led to complications with Ireland's ratification of the Maastricht Treaty. The Irish Government had succeeded in having a Protocol (later amended in a Solemn Declaration) attached to the Treaty in which the European Union formally recognized the Irish prohibition against abortion. However, the Attorney General's court order against "X" was overturned by the Irish Supreme Court, which ruled that abortion should be allowed in Ireland where there was a "real and substantial risk" to a woman's life. "X" had threatened suicide (a "real and substantial risk" to her life) and subsequently did have an abortion in England. The Constitutional prohibition against abortion was later modified by referendum, in November 1992. Two of the proposed constitutional amendments —guaranteeing pregnant women's freedom to travel abroad and limited rights to the circulation of information about abortion services—were voted into the Constitution in this referendum. A third amendment, proposing a more limited right to abortion than that already allowed by the Supreme Court, was rejected.

Two years later, Irish women's right to abortion is still extremely unclear. Although it is now lawful under the terms of the Supreme Court judgment in "X" for a woman to have an abortion where there is a "real and substantial risk" to her life, in fact, no abortions are known to have taken place in Ireland (Murphy-Lawless 1993; Smyth 1992; Whitty 1993).

The abortion controversy needs to be placed in the context of the Republic of Ireland's pride in being a modern democratic state. Independence from Britain was achieved in 1921, and the 1937 Constitution states that "all citizens shall, as human persons, be held equal before the law." Since the late 1950s, the economy has grown rapidly and, although relatively poor by comparison with other Western European countries, Ireland is currently ranked at twenty-one on the United Nations Human Development Index. Ireland is a member of the United Nations and a signatory to the Convention on the Elimination of all Forms of Discrimination Against Women (among other UN Conventions). It became a member of the then European Community in 1972, and a signatory to the European Convention on Human Rights.

The process of modernization and rapid economic growth, world recession notwithstanding, have brought about many changes, not the least of which is a marked if uneven tendency towards liberalization in social attitudes and behaviors (Whelan 1993). The culmination of Ireland's move towards modernization might be said to have occurred in 1990, when (and somewhat to Ireland's own surprise) a woman—Mary Robinson, a lawyer recognized as the prime champion in Ireland of social and civil rights for women and for marginalized groups generally—was elected as President (Smyth 1992a). Ireland has a vibrant Women's Movement with hundreds of active women's groups throughout the country and women's studies programs in most of the universities.

But is Ireland, for all that, a modern European state? The European dimension, however we cut it—geographically, politically, socially, culturally, economically—is not in doubt. Ireland is part of the European Union. No getting away from it. It is an immovable feast—and I use the word "feast" advisedly. Ireland has had a bonanza of funding from the EU for a variety of economic, infrastructural, and social projects, so even if it could extract itself politically from the EU, I doubt that it would want to renounce the cash benefits. But does the cash necessarily make the country more modern? Or more precisely, while some aspects of modernization are welcomed and financed, are others willfully obstructed and restricted? Reproductive rights is a key area in enabling us to see the (imposed) limits of modernization and of the benefits of European membership for women.

"The women themselves, they just don't come into it"

> *It's all facts and medical terminology, the women themselves, they don't come into it.*

> (Interviewee cited by Fletcher 1993, 46)

Women's struggle for reproductive self-determination occurs in the much broader framework of the feminist movement, as complex in Ireland as elsewhere in the West. Irish women have fought for and achieved rights and autonomy in many areas over the past two decades. The aims of the very first manifesto of the Irish Women's Liberation Movement (IWLM) in 1970 included: equal rights in law; equal pay; social welfare equality for women as single parents; equal educational opportunities, and contraception as a human right. All of these aims are now wholly or partly incorporated in Irish law and social policy, which does not mean, of course, that they are fully implemented in practice.

Alongside the first tentative mention by Irishwomen United (IU) of "the right of all women to self-determined sexuality," issues concerning violence came on the agenda in the mid-1970s. Irish law now recognizes rape within marriage as a criminal offense, and levels of awareness and information in relation to battery and sexual abuse have increased, although provision and funding for support services remains piecemeal and is nowhere adequate to meet women's needs. Employment equality legislation was introduced in the mid-1970s, although the gap between women's and men's average earnings is approximately 30 percent.[1] Even now, a new Equal Status Bill to prohibit discrimination on the basis of sexuality, age, and ethnicity is being drafted. In an atypically radical move by the legislators, the Unfair Dismissals Act was recently amended so that dismissal on the grounds of sexual orientation is now illegal. However, in a cruel twist of the legislative screw, shortly after the amendment had been introduced, its grave shortcomings were revealed when a young lesbian lost her job expressly because of her sexuality and failed on appeal to the Labour Court to be reinstated because she had been in the job for less than six months.

There are indeed many ways in which the everyday realities of Irish life give the lie to the shiny image of progress and modernism. This is abundantly clear in the steep unemployment rate, estimated at 17 percent, in the persistence of poverty, and in the area of women's rights and freedoms. For although Irish women have a long and impressive history of struggle against patriarchal control, resistance to change in women's status and roles remains fierce. Feminist "gains" are consistently undermined through sins of omission and commission, by failures of nerve as much as by overt assaults.

In Ireland, citizenship rights and social needs taken for granted elsewhere in the West continue to be construed as "moral issues"— and legally denied. To take one of the more dramatic examples of Irish traditionalism, divorce is still prohibited by the Constitution.* In a 1986 referendum, the Irish electorate voted against the introduction of divorce, although the number of people whose marriages had definitively ended was conservatively estimated to be about 72,000 at that time and there was widespread public demand for its introduction (Prendiville 1988). When the Government declared it

1. The introduction of employment equality legislation is commonly attributed to the impact of EC membership and the Employment Equality Directives. However, demands for employment equality had been forcefully articulated by Irish feminists and by the mainstream First Commission on the Status of Women in the early 1970s. In fact, when Ireland requested a derogation from the EC Commission for the implementation of the first Equality Directive, it was the campaigning pressure of the Women's Movement and of women in the trades unions which forced the Government to implement the Directives (Smyth 1993).

*See note on page 130.

would hold another referendum on divorce in the autumn of 1994, the "Masterminds of the Right" (O'Reilly 1991) immediately moved to turn the tide of public opinion—which had swung significantly in favor of divorce after the shameful debacle of the 1986 referendum—by deliberately guilt-tripping, manipulating, and panicking the electorate into rejecting divorce yet again. In an apocalyptic rallying-cry to his anti-divorce troops, the Archbishop of Dublin— the most powerful Catholic voice in the State—warned that "divorce is radically anti-social," and detrimental to the social good: "If, under the influence of the contraceptive culture, society accepts a view of marriage that releases the married couple from all commitment to procreation, it opens the way to the final debasement of marriage, the recognition of so-called homosexual marriages" (Dr. Desmond Connell in Coughlan 1994). A more profoundly reactionary, misogynistic, and homophobic ideology would be difficult to imagine.

The divorce referendum is now on hold while the High Court hears a challenge, initiated by the extreme-right, to the terms of the Judicial Separation Act, a crucial basis for the drafting of divorce legislation. This setback follows on the Supreme Court's rejection of the Government's Matrimonial Homes Bill (on the disposition of property in the event of divorce), also a major plank in divorce legislation. In a distinctly cautious ruling, the Supreme Court declared that the Bill would be a constitutionally impermissible invasion into the authority of the family (Newman 1994).

The divorce issue demonstrates some of the difficulties involved in working for social change in Ireland. It is clear that even a government expressly committed to introducing divorce is reluctant to take on the powerful right-wing lobby groups which now front extensively for the Catholic Church. The lessening of direct intervention by the Church hierarchy in matters of "public morality" should not be taken for acquiescence or indifference, even less for powerlessness. The Church retains a major hold on the key ideological bases of State policy through the education system, the pulpit, the Medical Council, and myriad lay organizations of "foot soldiers" which promulgate its theology/ideology in every corner of Irish society. The Catholic Church is still a huge bogey, whether in relation to divorce, abortion, or any progressive issue (see Inglis 1987).

What also emerges, when thinking about the struggle for women's liberation over the past two decades, is that while Irish feminists (of many persuasions) have looked to the law to provide a framework for freedom and enhanced citizenship, traditionalists have been able to use the law as an effective means of thwarting those very same freedoms. Most social analysts (including feminist analysts) place a positive value on the role of the higher courts in enabling the introduction or implementation of equality for women. However, on closer examination, the reality proves to be rather more volatile and inconsistent (Connelly 1993).

Typically, when the judgments delivered by Irish courts have been unsatisfactory or unworkable, the tendency has been to turn to the European courts for more liberal interpretations. There is no doubt that in many instances (and notably in relation to the decriminalization of male homosexuality), this strategy has yielded beneficial, if slow, results. In the case of abortion, however, the situation is much less clear-cut. The unsatisfactory or frankly inadequate outcomes of appeals to the European courts have less to do with differences between national and transnational legal and judicial systems than with the patriarchal construction and practice of law throughout the West.

Of course, resistance to the introduction of divorce and reproductive freedom for women might be interpreted as nothing more sinister than the anomalies—the inevitable residual undertow—of a society belatedly coming to terms with the end of the twentieth century and finding itself mortifyingly out of step with a "modern" European Union. There is some truth in this: there is an inevitable sense of disarray, insecurity, and fear as the old certainties are knocked down, one after another, like so many coconut shies at a fair. But the fears need to be confronted, not allowed to grow unchecked into a roaring flame of fanaticism and "moral panic" through political cowardice, inertia, or ineptitude at either (or both) the national or European levels. This, however, is precisely what has been *allowed* to happen.

I would suggest that a deliberate politics of inertia and ineptitude is pursued in Ireland and in and through the institutions of the EU as a means of reinforcing the status quo and, specifically, of ensuring that power remains concentrated in the hands of an elite ruling group of middle-aged, middle-class white males.[2]

---

2. The role of the EU and of its individual Member States in the Bosnian conflict bears witness to the tragic consequences of a politics of inertia and ineptitude. To interpret such a politics as deliberate is to suggest that European decision makers care only for their own interests; not to do so is to suggest that they are *really* stupid and incompetent.

"If I could have talked"

> *I still feel guilty about it and there's not a day goes by that I*
> *don't think about it and I spend time every day ... and I*
> *mean it's five years and I still cry, but I think that the crying*
> *could have stopped if I could have talked and I never could ...*
>
> (Interviewee cited by Fletcher 1993, 19)

The voices of the countless thousands of Irish women who have
had abortions have been condemned to silence. For the past two
decades, Ireland has been noisily embattled over the ownership of
women's reproducing bodies and, since 1983, specifically over the
issue of abortion. Yet, in all that long time, the numbers of women
who have been able to say publicly that they have had an abortion
can be counted on the fingers of one hand. Further, I can personally vouch for the dangers involved in being publicly identified
with pro-abortion/pro-choice politics, as can many other Irish
feminists (Riddick interviewed by Fletcher 1993, 38; Smyth 1992b;
Smyth forthcoming).

Where abortion remains unutterable for the vast majority of people, it is not surprising that the experience cannot be talked about:
there is no available vocabulary for doing so and—just as importantly—no way of hearing whatever words might be found to break
through the obfuscating sound barriers of moral judgment and con-
demnation. During the 1992 abortion controversies and campaigns,
abortion was (as is the case elsewhere) consistently referred to by
anti-abortionists as "murder," "assassination," and "atrocity": not
only was abortion not named, its unspeakability was deliberately
reinforced through a tactic which consisted in metaphorizing/ meta-
morphosing it from a physical experience and social reality into a
moral "debate," a juridic-medical "problem," and a criminal offense.
Given these imposed meanings, to declare that you had had an
abortion, or that you favored the provision of abortion, produced
exactly the same effect as declaring yourself a murderer, a criminal,
and a social pariah.[3]

One of the most effective silencing tactics has been that of the
powerful Medical Council, which represents the medical profession

---

3. In fact, I find it hard to write about abortion in an "academic" context because
of the difficulty of distancing myself from the pain and desperation and because the
evacuation from "proper" academic discourse of personal experience and emotions
is so utterly antithetical to my understanding of feminist values and politics.

and, very importantly, determines the ethical guidelines for Irish medical practice. Precisely echoing Catholic Church teaching, the Medical Council has argued, since 1983, that when a pregnancy is terminated in a case of uterine cancer or in an ectopic pregnancy, this does not constitute "abortion" but something else. In 1993, the Council published guidelines on abortion in which it was stated that doctors who performed abortions in Ireland would be acting unethically and would be opened to a charge of misconduct. The authority of the Medical Council to issue such guidelines has been widely contested. However, a year later, the Council was still advancing one of the major arguments it had used during the referenda campaign, that is, "the necessity for abortion to preserve the life or health of the sick mother remains to be proved" (Hegarty 1994). Thus, the Medical Council never has to name abortion, because (a) it is always actually something else, which is, in any case, (b) unnecessary.

These are tactics with which pro-abortion activists elsewhere are all too wearily familiar (see for example, Delphy 1993; Franklin 1991; Goggin 1993; Hoff 1994; McNeil 1991). As a weapon in the Irish anti-abortion arsenal, they have been peculiarly successful because they merge seamlessly into the Catholic anti-sex, anti-woman puritanism of the ideological foundations of the Irish State, as expressly articulated in the Constitution and in social legislation. The efficacy of such tactics can be measured by the unwillingness of government and politicians to use the "A" word in any circumstances. Throughout its own 1992 referenda campaign, the Government systematically substituted the phrase "the substantive issue," first used by the Supreme Court in its ruling in the "X" case, for the word "abortion." This bizarre Unofficial Secrets Act meant that although the entire population knew perfectly well that thousands of Irish women go to Britain every year to have abortions, the reality was never spoken in so many words, but only ever referred to in code. Tactics, weapons, secrets, and codes: you could be forgiven for thinking the people of Ireland were at war. As indeed they were.[4]

In a speech made shortly before the 1992 Referenda, I put it (polemically) thus:

> Abortion has been disappeared, spirited away, out of language and reality altogether, and with it the countless numbers of women who have had them, are having them and will continue to have them,

---

4. I am well aware of the resonances of the term "war" in the context of Ireland. However, people's (women's) lives are *also* destroyed by ideological warfare.

whatever the law dictates. Let us now say the word—the A word—slowly, clearly, carefully—just to see how it feels on our unaccustomed tongues: ABORTION. That is what Irish women go to Britain to have. They don't go to have a good time, they don't go to commit a crime, they don't go because they want to go, and as we all know perfectly well, they certainly don't go to have a "substantive issue": they go to Britain to have that forbidden word, that unmentionable reality, that inadmissible experience, that unlawful necessity—an ABORTION. They go because they have to go, because their needs and their rights as women and as citizens are denied them by the Irish Constitution and by Irish Statute law.[5]

In a culturally specific twist to this linguistic transubstantiation of abortion, defying the code by naming the reality came to be construed as a peculiarly "un-Irish" activity and even as "anti-women" and anti-European. In 1991, the Irish Government had succeeded in having a special Protocol inserted in the Maastricht Treaty guaranteeing that European law could never override Article 40.3.3 of the Constitution—the notorious 8th Amendment which guarantees "the right to life of the unborn." One of the outcomes of the "X" case in 1992 had been the discovery of this Protocol, which the Government had "failed" to publicize. Once the public understood the meaning of the Protocol, the Government was forced to back-pedal and, after bizarre and intricate negotiations, a Solemn Declaration was appended to the Protocol, purporting to reduce its effect. However, it has been argued that the Declaration, and probably the Protocol itself, have no binding status in law (Reid 1992; see also Whitty 1993). Given the draconian anti-abortion Protocol, the pro-choice movement logically called for a "No" vote in the referendum to ratify the Maastricht Treaty (in June 1992) on the grounds that ratification would effectively constitute acceptance of the State's right to deny women abortion. However, the influential Council for the Status of Women, which had adopted a cautiously pro-choice stance, urged a "Yes" vote on the grounds that the Treaty was important to the European Union and that Europe had proved its importance to women—not least in its financing of women's projects through the NOW (New Horizons for Women) program. The implication was unmistakable: in voting against the Treaty, Irish women would be voting against their own best interests, although in point of fact, voting in favor of the Treaty ensured that repressive Irish law overrode the EU in the matter of abortion.

5. Speech made at the launch of *The Abortion Papers: Ireland*, Dublin, October 1992.

An important strand in extreme-right ideology and politics in Ireland since the 1970s has been the emphasis on Ireland as the last bastion of moral and sexual purity and of the traditional family in the Western world. In this scenario, Ireland plays the heroic role of the tiny beleaguered State staunchly defending the Faith of Our Fathers[6] (and the invisibility of our mothers) by holding out against the global wave of depravity which threatens to engulf it, and thus (somewhat illogically) Ireland shines as a beacon for all those in need of salvation. The speeches of Pope John Paul II during his 1979 visit to Ireland, frequently invoked in the 1983 and 1992 abortion campaigns and in the 1986 divorce campaign, reinforced this Armageddon-like image and encouraged "Ireland" to see itself as a tiny but stalwart bastion of traditional Catholic values:

> Your country seems in a sense to be living again the temptations of Christ. Satan, The Tempter, the adversary of Christ, will use all his might and all his deception to win Ireland for the way of the world (Pope John Paul II in Prendiville 1988, 360).

Those—especially women—who go the way of all flesh and "choose" divorce, contraception, or abortion are therefore traitors to both Church and State.

The message is that Ireland must and *can* save the world from dissolution and destruction. This would be merely ludicrous if it did not so wittingly appeal to a need for status and self-importance in the collective Irish psyche. For whatever Irish people may like to think, the fact is that Ireland is an insignificant geographical, economic, and political entity in the European and, *a fortiori*, global scheme of things.[7] However for an ex-colonial state, with an insecure sense of national identity, exacerbated by the geographical proximity of its ex-colonizers and by their economic, linguistic, and cultural dominance, as well as that of Europe and the United States more generally, this is not at all an easy fact to accept. The tendency towards self-aggrandizement is pertinent in the context of the strengthening and expansion of the European Union as a political force.

---

6. This is the title of a widely known Irish Catholic hymn in which religious belief and nationalism are inextricably intertwined.

7. Small does not equal simple. This point needs to be made because Ireland is persistently caricatured as small-therefore-backward-and-stupid by the international media. Of course Ireland's abortion situation is stupid. However, a nation's legislation is stupid not because that nation is small, but because the legislation is stupid.

There is much talk in Ireland of "our role in Europe," accompanied by uncertainty about what this is, or can be, and some difficulty in communicating it to Ireland's European "partners." Ireland's need for a specific "role" (a *raison d'être*) is understandable but disturbing when one of the chief ways, de facto, it has achieved a distinctive identity within Europe is through its denial to women of full citizenship rights.

As the recent cases of infanticide make so tragically clear, the process of modernization is underscored by tensions, confusions, and contradictions, which leave deliberate and indelible scars on women's lives. Sexuality and reproduction are the arenas where the struggle between the forces of conservatism and of modernization, and increasingly the definition of citizenship, is fought with particular ferocity. This has been, and continues to be, the painful experience of women in Ireland, an experience which no amount of European Unionizing seems able or willing to change. The absorption—to the point of obsession—of the entire country in the abortion controversy of 1992 signals the extent to which people widely, if sometimes obscurely, perceive abortion as a defining or "boundary" issue for the society and culture as a whole (Smyth 1992). Succinctly, what underlay a significant part of the abortion debate was the substance and meaning of Ireland's distinctive identity: introducing abortion would make Ireland more like the rest of the EU member states—and therefore less distinctively "Irish."

The silencing of women who have had abortions and/or who are active in pro-abortion politics must, of course, be placed in the context of the specific construction of motherhood in Ireland. Historically, the experiences of women who were impregnated without benefit of a marriage certificate were not simply unrecorded; they were strenuously denied and deeply buried. Such women were "unspeakable" (and thus unspeaking) and the legal status of their children was concretely less than that of children born to married parents. The denial which stigmatized "unmarried mothers" lasted well into the later decades of this century. Although attitudes, laws, and social welfare policies have changed significantly since the 1970s when feminists began to expose and challenge the hypocrisy and injustice of the treatment of single women raising children, the renewed emphasis at the present time on "The Family," and the insistent representation of "The Family" as comprising a married Daddy and Mummy with (at least) two perfectly "legitimate" (and perfect) children is once again tending to make the real social status of unmarried mothers problematic. In Irish judicial interpretation,

"The Family" is construed as that based on marriage, in accordance with the Constitution which designates it as the "base unit of society." The fact is that the married motherhood imperative continues to be the 11th Commandment for Irish women and that any and every challenge to its dominance is resisted. But in the 1990s, Irish women are not to be thwarted in their determination to achieve autonomy and freedom. The socio-sexual behavior of Irish women has undergone the most profound changes over the past two decades with contraception widely practiced and far more women now seeking to remain in the labor force following marriage and children. Average family size has fallen by half in the past twenty-five years, while births to single mothers have risen dramatically from 3 percent of all births in 1973 to 19.5 percent in 1993. At least 4,500 Irish women obtain abortions every year—by traveling to Britain, which has served as an "escape-valve" for the problem of abortion in Ireland since the introduction of the relatively liberal UK 1967 Abortion Act.

But as women's willingness to serve the patriarchal family conspicuously decreases, the pressures on them to do so are dramatically increasing. Childcare is not provided either by the State or by the private sector in any numerically significant way. There are still no sex education programs in schools, although the present Minister for Education (a woman) has stated her intention of introducing such programs in the near future. How the Catholic Church will respond to this move remains to be seen, but we can be certain that it will not happen without an entirely unholy row.

"I was just in a desperate situation"

I wasn't exercising a right or a choice or anything. I was just in a desperate situation.

(Interviewee in Fletcher 1993, 43)

Control of women's sexuality and reproduction has been high on the Irish political agenda since the foundation of the State. The "X" case and subsequent abortion referenda were therefore in no sense a bolt from the blue, whatever the views of the Euro and global media. The situation which emerged in 1992 was the logical and sadly predictable consequence of a labyrinthine history of lobbying by powerful interest groups (chief among them the Catholic Church) and of legislative and constitutional moves designed to maintain women in reproductive bondage which had been gathering momentum since the late 1970s.

Throughout the 1970s and 1980s, feminists had fought a long and complicated battle for the right to contraception (Barry 1992; Murphy-Lawless 1993); and, although contraceptives were to become progressively more available in legislative fits and starts during those decades, it was not until the summer of 1993 that legal restrictions on the sale of condoms were removed. Tellingly, the contraceptive battle was ultimately won not because the State had finally recognized women's right to control their fertility, but because of the spread of AIDS. In fact, to enable the sale of condoms "over the counter," the Government had to "exclude them from the legal definition of contraceptives" (Whitty 1993).

The energy-consuming difficulty of the struggle for contraceptive rights and the "escape-valve" of the well-worn abortion route to Britain (see Conroy Jackson 1992) partly explain why abortion was not an issue in the Women's Movement in Ireland during the 1970s. However, its absence from the feminist agenda during this period also indicates the extent to which it was experienced as a deeply "taboo" issue in a country still subject to Rome Rule. By 1979, when a small "Right to Choose" group formed in Dublin, the Church and its front-line lay troops were already preparing to launch a major offensive against the rising tide of feminist-led change (O'Reilly 1991).

For the next decade and more—and who knows now for how much longer—Irish society was to be dominated by virulent public controversy over the issue of abortion rights. Framed at either end by the deeply divisive and disruptive abortion referenda of 1983 and 1992, those years were horrendously marked by a number of shameful cases in which individual women were scapegoated and sacrificed in the bitter war waged by the forces of conservatism against women's sexual and reproductive autonomy (see for example, McCafferty 1985).

Even after the anti-abortion movement had "won" the referendum of 1983, and the prohibition against abortion (already illegal under the Offenses Against the Persons Act 1861) had been "copperfastened" by the Constitutional amendment, opponents pursued the Family Planning and Counseling services and others through the courts until they achieved a total ban against the dissemination of information about abortion services outside the country.

Two major abortion information cases were taken by SPUC (Society for the Protection of Unborn Children) who sought injunctions to prevent two counseling centers from providing nondirective pregnancy counseling (*Open Door*). They also sought an injunction preventing students' union officers (*Grogan*) from disseminating information about abortion services outside the country. These cases were heard in the Irish higher courts and were referred or appealed to the two European Courts: *Grogan* was referred to the European Court of Justice (ECJ) by Justice Carroll of the High Court, while *Open Door* was appealed to the European Court of Human Rights (ECHR).[8] Although the bases and reasons were different in each case, there was to be no immediate comfort, and no information, for Irish women on foot of the European Courts' rulings. In the case of *Grogan* (1991), the ECJ "reaffirmed that Irish laws banning abortion were not within the scope of Community law," although the Court also held "that the medical termination of pregnancy was an economic service within the meaning of the EC Treaty." However, "since the students in the case were third parties who had no economic interest in the matter (i.e., were not themselves seeking an abortion), the ECJ held that they had no Community law right to distribute information" (Reid 1992).

The ECHR case is rather more complicated, partly because although the Court's rulings are not binding on Irish courts, its findings are always publicized and its case law is influential for the ECJ. Eventually, the ECHR ruled in *Open Door* (1992) that Ireland was in breach of Article 10 of the European Convention on Human Rights, to which Ireland is a signatory. One of the counseling centers involved (the Dublin Well Woman Centre) then applied to the Irish Supreme Court to have the order preventing them from conducting nondirective pregnancy counseling services lifted. However, in the summer of 1994, the Supreme Court declined to do so in a four-to-one majority ruling, on the technical grounds that the Supreme Court was not the appropriate court to make such decisions. The only woman member of the Supreme Court, Mrs. Justice Susan Denham, gave the dissenting judgment.

---

8. The European Court of Justice (ECJ) in Luxembourg is the supreme court of Community law. Its rulings are binding on EU Member States. The European Court of Human Rights (ECHR) in Strasbourg is the court of the European Convention on Human Rights. Although its findings cannot be enforced in Irish law, its rulings are considered influential (see Reid 1992).

So, what about women's rights, women's lives? "The women themselves, they don't come into it." Women are there to be batted around, from court to court, and referendum to referendum. As the court cases continued in Ireland and in Europe, the "X" case occurred, followed swiftly by the revelation of the Maastricht Protocol, the insertion of the Solemn Declaration, and the Maastricht referendum, discussed above. Then, in November 1992, the second referendum on abortion rights was held. Technically, this was actually three referenda as the electorate was asked to vote on three new amendments to the Constitution, phrased as follows:

12th Amendment
It shall be unlawful to terminate the life of an unborn unless such termination is necessary to save the life, as distinct from the health, of the mother where there is an illness or disorder of the mother giving rise to a real and substantial risk to her life, not being a risk of self-destruction.

13th Amendment
Subsection 3 of this section shall not limit freedom to travel between the State and another state.

14th Amendment
Subsection 3 of this section shall not limit freedom to obtain or make available, in the State, subject to such conditions as may be laid down by law, information relating to services lawfully available in another state.

Calling for a "yes" vote in all three cases, the Government claimed that the result of the referendum would "decide whether Article 40.3.3 of the Constitution is to be amended, in relation to three separate issues—the Right to Life, Travel, and Information." Their objective in trying to resolve what they called "an extremely difficult problem" was

to do what is right in the public interest, motivated by deep concern for the right to life of women and also fully committed to the protection of the right to life of the unborn. There is no human right more fundamental or more important than the right to life (*The Referendums on The Right to Life, Travel, and Information: Key Questions and Answers,* Government Information Publication, November 1992).

The Alliance for Choice, representing feminist, student, and political groupings as well as "front-line" services, formed after the long-delayed Government announcement of the referendum wording.

The Alliance campaigned for a "yes" vote on the issues of travel and information (13th and 14th amendments) as absolute minimum requirements while stressing the scandal of having to vote for them at all in a supposedly "democratic" and "modern" state. The meaning and effect of the 12th amendment—the so-called "substantive issue"—inevitably generated widespread confusion and intense controversy. The Alliance for Choice firmly opposed this amendment. In a pre-referendum information leaflet, the Alliance commented:

> [...] you will be asked to vote on a new clause (i.e., the 12th amendment) which will once again tamper with the rights of pregnant women. The courts have said that women have the right to abortion in Ireland when their lives are at risk, including the risk of suicide. The Government proposals are designed to overturn the court decision on suicide. They also want to ensure that a pregnant woman's health cannot be taken into account when a decision on pregnancy termination is being made. A woman's health is just as important as her life.

In the outcome, over 60 percent of the electorate approved the amendments on travel and information, while 65 percent voted "no" to the 12th amendment, proposing a highly circumscribed right to abortion. Both pro-choice and anti-abortion groups claimed the result as a victory. Given the complexity of the triple referendum, the results are difficult to interpret precisely. However, while the "no" vote on the abortion rights issue clearly included a sizable proportion of "hard-line" anti-abortion voters, it was also the case that the "yes" vote on this issue included voters who were persuaded by Government and politicians that a favorable vote would mean more extensive abortion options for women. The Alliance for Choice argued that the three votes—"no, yes, yes"—demonstrated that the Irish electorate had rejected the extremism of the anti-abortion lobby, and were calling for a humane response to the causes and consequences of crisis pregnancies. This interpretation was reinforced by pre-referendum opinion polls and surveys which had shown that a majority of Irish people believed that abortion should be available when the life or health of the mother was at risk, and in cases of rape or incest.

The results of the General Election, held on the same day, in which the highest ever number of women (12 percent) and of Labour TDs (MPs) were elected (the Labour Party is now in a coalition government), also indicated a clear desire for change and for a more left-liberal ethos in Irish politics and society.

The Government has said it intends to introduce legislation on the "control of information relating to foreign abortion services,"[9] although the constitutionality of such legislation is contested by feminists and service providers.[10] The only "right" to abortion in Ireland still rests on the Supreme Court judgment in the case of "X," about which there has been no follow-up legislation. In the course of the Supreme Court's judgment in the "X" case, the then Government was severely taken to task for its failure to legislate following the 1983 referendum (McDonagh 1993). The present Government appears to be heading in exactly the same direction, that is, straight for a large hole in the sand. Meanwhile, an estimated 4,500 Irish women still have to head for Britain to obtain an abortion. I believe that while the Government may move to introduce (superfluous and insulting) legislation to control information *if* the divorce referendum is carried, it will seek to postpone indefinitely the task of legislating on the circumstances under which abortions may be carried out in Ireland.

Irish women are left, still and for the foreseeable future, in no-citizen's land.

Toward a Conclusion: Ireland—Backwards, Forwards, or in the Same Place?

It is clear that the sorry state of abortion affairs in Ireland raises complex questions about the modus operandi of the European Union and its relations with the Member States and, crucially and urgently, about the meaning of European citizenship for women in particular.

I think it is important to ask *not* "Is Europe good for women?", which is probably unanswerable in its simplifying generality, but rather "Has membership in the European Union proved useful to women in Ireland in the specific case of abortion?" To which the only answer is "no." Granted, the problem was of Ireland's own making to begin with, but "Europe" has failed to provide workable solutions for women trapped in second-class citizenship within its

---

9. Letter to the author from the Minister for Health, 5 May 1994.

10. I am greatly indebted to Ruth Riddick, Education Officer of the Irish Family Planning Association and pro-choice activist of long standing, for drawing my attention to this and to several other points (Letter to author, 22 June 1994).

boundaries. The issue of Irish abortion rights thus highlights several important and troubling aspects of the European Union's treatment of women's citizenship rights:

(1) *The limited ambit and meaning of European Union.* As Madeleine Reid has pointed out:

> Community law's relevance to abortion is limited. Its main preoccupation is with the economic law of the market, and not with social, moral or health issues; it sees these as remaining a matter for the individual states (1992, 29).

In fact, Member States appear to have a very wide or even total margin of discretion with regard to these issues. The Advocate General of the ECJ declared, in the Court's interim hearing on the Irish student unions information case (*Grogan* 1991), that an EU public policy clause permits individual states full discretion in matters of a "moral and philosophical nature which affect the fundamental interests of society" (Murphy-Lawless, 1993).

What the Advocate General refers to as the "fundamental interests of society" was, in the Irish case, the fundamental denial to women of equal treatment and full citizenship in that men are not constrained by any similar measures in relation to their reproductive capacity.

(2) *The uneasy and unclear relation between national and transnational legislative and judicial systems.* This emerged with particular force over the Maastricht Protocol, where Ireland was "allowed" a derogation which it may well not have been within the EU's power to grant. At present, it appears that where no issue of economic or market interest is involved, the EU is not overly concerned about Member States' conduct of their "social" affairs. For example, in the brief section dealing with "Women's Rights and Opportunities" in the EU Green Paper on Social Policy (1993), "women" are represented primarily as workers, although as Conroy Jackson has pointed out (1992), the male model of work which is at the core of the Treaty of Rome and of EU policy as a whole has very little relevance for the majority of women and is decreasingly meaningful for many men.

(3) *The "Democratic Deficit."* It is important to note the relatively weak role of the European Parliament in this respect: the only democratically elected body within the EU structures has had no real power to affect EU policy. One of the effects of the Maastricht Treaty will be to attribute wider powers to the Parliament, but it

remains to be seen how this will be interpreted in practice. At present, the EU can hardly be called a participatory democracy.

(4) *The cumbersome mechanisms and bureaucracy of the EU institutions* which, in relation to the issue of abortion, could have literally fatal consequences. A particular problem here is that the caseload of the ECJ is now so high that cases can take up to eighteen months to be heard, and (unlike pregnancy) there is a similarly slow rate of delivery for court rulings (Reid 1992). There is no question of the EU offering "quick solutions" to anyone. As Elizabeth Meehan laconically comments: "[I]t is possible to argue that neither the [ECJ] nor Member States can or want to make fundamental alterations to the material basis of women's citizenship" (1993, 116).

People (women and men) also feel alienated from the bureaucratic and legalistic procedures and language of the EU. The European Union could not be described as a "popular" institution, not least because it has made no attempt to appeal to the imagination of its citizens.

(5) *The patriarchal construction of citizenship* obtains as strongly within EU institutions as it does within individual Member States. While the EU generally adopts a more "liberal" rhetoric and stance than the Irish State on matters of public policy (including equality issues), the net result is identical from both sources: no material change. The more liberal discourse of the ECJ in relation to the abortion information case did not result in an easier and more informed situation for Irish women. The technical and legal exigencies of the EU are frequently proffered as an *explanation* for its failure to deliver on social issues, to which I think women must answer: this will not do. Randall (1992) points to the tendency of politicians to "depoliticize" abortion by redefining it as a primarily technical and administrative matter. This has certainly been the experience of Irish women within both the Irish and the EU juridic-legal systems.

The main reason why the EU is not "useful" for women on the pivotal issue of reproductive rights is precisely because these rights are a cornerstone of the patriarchal edifice. While a more liberal Europe (i.e., more liberal than Ireland) may offer a measure of relief to some women, it is not, for all that, less patriarchal. When one reflects on the abortion situation both within Ireland and in the EU context, what emerges most clearly is the manifest inappropriateness of the law as a means of addressing women's reproductive needs. The law, in every single instance, both Irish and European, is used or called upon to *regulate* and *control* women's reproduction.

Appeals to the law in respect of reproduction are always about *who* has the power to control women's sexuality. Given that the legal and judicial systems as we know them in Europe are patriarchal in their philosophy and history, and heavily male-dominated in terms of their personnel, feminists should not be optimistic about the ability of that system to provide substantially and consistently greater freedoms for women.[11] The European Commission has resolutely resisted any and all attempts to have violence against women (except in the employment-based case of sexual harassment) incorporated in policy and thinking about European citizens' rights.

No more than the Irish State, "Europe" has not provided a solution to the Irish abortion problem. However, unless one is to withdraw altogether from "the State" (which is a material impossibility) or to adopt (or return to) anarchist politics, the only way to move towards a more beneficial situation for women is to set about creating a "Europe" where freedoms will be concrete, specific, and guaranteed for everyone.

Ireland is atypical within the EU in that it is the only state which still prohibits abortion in law.[12] This is a problem for *all* women in Europe and not just for Irish women. For if Irish women do not have full citizenship rights at present in Ireland, neither do they have them in the EU, despite the principles of equality enunciated in the Irish Constitution, in the Treaty of Rome, and in subsequent European documents. If Irish women, who are also European, do not currently enjoy full citizenship rights, they must question the will and the ability of the EU to respect the citizenship rights of *all* European women.

Not long ago, I attended a conference in Paris organized by a French coordinating group and ENWRAC (European Network for Women's Rights to Abortion and Contraception). What struck me

---

11. Canada is the only state in the West where abortion is not subject to legal regulation (Brodie, Gavigan and, Jenson 1992). There is a powerful argument to be made for the "deregulation" of abortion rights in EU Member States.

12. In February 1995, with no prior warning, the Irish Government introduced the Regulation of Information (Services Outside State for Termination of Pregnancies) Bill. This highly restrictive Bill is likely to be enacted before the end of 1995. While it permits the provision of information about abortion services legally available in other countries by friends, doctors, and counselors, it prohibits a doctor or counselling agency from making appointments with abortion services abroad on behalf of a client/patient. The Bill also prohibits "advocacy" of abortion in print or visual media and the "unsolicited" distribution of information about abortion services (see Clarity 1995).

Following completion of this article, a referendum on the issue of divorce was held on 24 November 1995. The result was in favor of a limited form of divorce. The

first—and forcibly—was the extreme diversity of the law and practice of women's reproductive rights. Gradually, however, as women told their "national" stories, from France, Germany, Spain, Portugal, Poland, the Netherlands, Slovenia, Britain, and other European countries, other "evidence" emerged which was at least as important, although not comforting:

> *Nowhere* are abortion rights safe from the hostile and increasingly powerful attacks of the extreme right;
>
> *Nowhere* is women's access to abortion totally unproblematic;
>
> *Nowhere* in Europe is women's reproduction free from legal and/or medical control, as is the case for men.

What gave me much comfort and hope was the evidence that *everywhere* feminists are actively resisting constraints on the freedoms of all women and refusing to accept the minimum as anywhere near enough.

---

referendum was carried by 50.03 percent of the electorate (i.e., just over 9,000 votes). At the time of going to press, the anti-divorce campaign has indicated that it may take a constitutional action challenging this result on the basis of government expenditure in favor of a "yes" vote during the campaign. This note itself indicates how difficult it is to further a more open and feminist agenda in the Irish state.

9

The Common Market of Violence

Jalna Hanmer

Women's relationship to the state is of fundamental importance in creating the conditions under which violence against women both occurs and can be ameliorated.[1] In Europe, this relationship is an issue at the level of the individual nation states as well as that of the European Union. The nature of the individual state, with its various departments and ways of delivering individual entitlements, affects how violence against women is dealt with, how women use state services, and how they experience the violence that is directed against them.[2] More importantly, the state's character influences women's ability to leave abusive men. A woman's ability to gain effective intervention from the state's statutory agencies depends also on the constructive involvement of others, including family, friends, and employers. There are important differences between and within European states, which contribute to the many reasons why ending a violent relationship may range from difficult to impossible, even

1. Violence from known men, i.e. husbands, co-habitees, and boyfriends, is the focus of this chapter. This violence can be physical, sexual, emotional, and economic. It may be directed against women exclusively or may include violence against their children and others for whom women may have responsibility, e.g., siblings.

2. In European countries, welfare provision is available through the state and includes housing, income maintenance, social work, and other social care. It may be administered locally, nationally, or a combination thereof. The criminal justice system may have elements of local or shared national and local administration, but its structures are generally sophisticated, and there is strong national direction and ultimate control. Centralized state control is common for services and individual entitlements. These patterns of organizing services are very different from those of the United States where such services may not exist or are provided by nonprofit organizations. Additionally, greater local control may be exercised throughout the American electoral system.

when the state assumes some responsibility for ensuring women's right to a life free from violence. Eliminating violence against women is no easy task; one often encounters societal resistance.

Unlike individual nation states, which seek to regulate the totality of individual and community life, the European Union is fundamentally an economic union; issues concerning family life and welfare are rarely addressed, which make it difficult to raise the issue of violence against women within European Union policy. Nonetheless, women have mobilized within numerous social and political arenas, thus expanding the theoretical location of violence against women through scholarship on citizenship and the links between violence and women's economic and social development. Enhanced understanding of these issues, together with the recognition of violence against women as a human rights violation, have led women into political activity throughout Europe and globally through the United Nations.

This article traces the development of how the issue of violence against women surfaced in Europe. It explores women's efforts both to escape from and move against such abuse while accounting for important obstacles to such endeavors. This discussion demonstrates how the state can shift positions, shattering any simplistic gendered notions of the state and the European Union. The examples in this article are drawn primarily from Britain and British research concerning the ways in which the state affects women's experiences of violence from the men they know. It was in Britain that the issue of violence against women was first politicized in Europe. Moreover, British research demonstrates important commonalities between women from different cultures and ethnic groups while also noting the ways in which states construct and maintain significant differences between women.

The Emergence of The Problem

In those European countries not experiencing open warfare, the central issue with violence against women is that the assailants of women are more likely to be known men than strangers (Elman and Eduards 1991; Mooney 1993). It is a fact that the violence directed towards women by men increases with the closeness of the relationship (Dobash and Dobash 1979; Smith 1989). Although women are also the victims of violence from men not known to them, statistically speaking, the problem is relatively minor. Nonetheless, it is this less common violence that is most likely to be acted upon by relevant state agencies throughout Europe.

The recognition of violence against women from the men known to them first occurred in Britain (England, Scotland, and Wales) and the Netherlands. The special events that created a climate where the problem became socially visible arose out of liberation struggles, especially women's liberation movements. These movements in Europe began at different times, and the initial focuses on types of violence against women varied. In France, for example, the first issue to be taken up, as in the United States, was rape.

In Britain and the Netherlands, the initial focus was on home based violence from husbands, co-habitees, and boyfriends. The family was conceptualized as a major site of women's oppression by women who first described themselves as belonging to the Women's Liberation Movement. Later, many of these same women would refer to themselves as radical feminists. Knowledge of this new issue and of refuges (i.e., battered women's shelters) was taken into the European political world through the International Tribunal on Crimes Against Women in Brussels in March 1976 (Russell and Van de Van 1976). Witnesses from Scotland, England, and the Netherlands testified to their experiences of violence from the men with whom they lived, the refusal of state agencies to help them, and the safety they found in refuges established by those in the Women's Liberation Movement. Through these Tribunal hearings, women from other European countries gained knowledge about this issue and were then inspired to set up refuges within their own countries. By 1976, there were groups organizing to aid battered women in Belgium, Denmark, France, Germany, Greece, Ireland, the Netherlands, and Switzerland (Warrior 1976). Outside Europe, Australia, Canada, Japan, and the United States were providing refuges, and Fiji, Mexico, and New Zealand were concerned and exploring the problem.

In Britain, the discovery of this issue arose out of consciousness-raising politics. Women were coming to the Women's Liberation Movement center in Goldhawk Road, London, where they talked about the mental, sexual, and physical violence they were enduring. This women's group decided to allow a woman and her children to stay in their premises, despite the fact that they had agreed with their landlord, the local council (i.e., the local government), that as designated slum clearance property it was not to be used for residential purposes. Because of the egalitarian style of organizing and decision-making processes in the Women's Liberation Movement, once one woman had stayed, it was impossible to deny any other the right to do so. News spread quickly and refuges were set up in almost all major cities in Britain by 1974.[3] That same year, Dutch women established a refuge in Amsterdam.

It is now more than twenty years since women in Europe first attempted to change patterns of social responses to women experiencing violence from known men. We must conclude that the societal resistance to change is very great; for while progress has been made, women's safety from male violence remains a major social problem throughout Europe. Each state within the European Union has its own history of struggle with violence against women. While there are many differences, there are also similarities.

State Responses to Violence Against Women

There are now measures to counter violence against women, however rudimentary, in all the European countries that comprise the Union. The issue is being raised on the local and national levels of these governments. The discussions have resulted in policies, provisions, and statutory agency interventions on behalf of women (d'Ancona 1984).

Although any married woman may have a violent husband, there are important differences between women that are created and maintained by the state. For example, a woman who enters Britain to marry a British citizen may not leave him in the first year unless she is prepared to be returned to her country of origin (European Women's Lobby 1995). Even if women are violently and abusively maltreated, only a political campaign on behalf of an individual woman has any chance of creating an exception to the enforcement of this policy. Further, racism permeates those state agencies charged with the responsibility for community and welfare provisions. Thus, not all women are equally responded to and assisted to the same degree (Hanmer 1994).

The question of why it is so problematic to challenge violence against women within individual nation-states was initially conceived

---

3. At this stage, the nineteenth-century knowledge of, and actions around, violence against women in the home remained unknown; women activists thought they had uncovered a completely new form of oppression of women. Jo Sutton, the first national coordinator of the National Women's Aid Federation, began the research into this past (1989).

in terms of the character of the male-dominated state (Hanmer 1982). The social construction of society into two distinctive spheres, the private and the public, is of fundamental importance, and the state, more recently the European Union, has a pivotal role in maintaining this division. A central problem is that power relations between women and men are considered to be private—off-limits to the involvement of others—unless such relations are constructed to occur in public, e.g., employment. The public, by contrast, is the realm of state regulation and intervention. The question then becomes: what factors can be used and what analysis is useful in attempts to reconstruct the private as public when the issue is violence against women from known men? While this is a practical problem for women working to end violence against women, it is also a theoretical challenge to feminism.

In their efforts to combat violence against women, feminists are confronted by two central paradoxes. First, women turn to men they know for protection from violence when these are the very men most likely to harm them. Second, in their attempts to leave abusive men, women turn to the very social organizations and state institutions that too often reinforce the false division of public and private in relation to violence against women from the men they know (Hanmer and Saunders 1984). This is complex; an early effort to demonstrate the way these processes intermesh focused on how women who seek to escape the men who abuse them are thrown back by state agencies upon these men for protection (Hanmer and Saunders 1984). Early conceptual presentations did not explore the nature of the state in any depth, but rather defined how women perceived violence, abuse, and harassment. Studies focused on the lack of assistance women received when they turn to state agencies for help.

Our early work in the 1980s led eventually to a study of policing in the geographical area of West Yorkshire, a county in England (Hanmer and Saunders 1993). This brought about an elaboration of the nature of the male-dominated state together with ways of making inroads into its service delivery. This research, analysis, and strategy disproved the popular but false notion that state power is monolithic in resistance as well as in its maintenance and pursuit of its own interests. The police of West Yorkshire accepted all the recommendations of the research and implemented them in a manner reminiscent of authoritarian organizations. Further, their efforts served as a national demonstration project and, while services for women from the police are uneven nationally and within individual police forces, some improvements have been made. The question then became, why did this happen? That is, what theory can explain the capacity of certain components of male-dominated states to deliver more appropriate services, particularly when these may restrict the capacity of men to control women by any means they choose?

It seems more likely that the state institution charged with the socially legitimated expression and control of violence interpreted their interests (i.e., organizational goals and system maintenance) differently, than they saw the error of their ways. This is not to deny the possibility that individuals within organizations may actively favor the delivery of direct and important women-friendly services any more than it denies that others within the same organization may remain opposed and recalcitrant to implementing such services. The argument, instead, is that in certain circumstances a consideration of system maintenance takes precedence over the desires of individuals.

As differences between men within organizations became apparent, so too did differences between women. For example, while some women oppose male domination, others may support forms of family life in which men are dominant. Women in relationships with violent men usually involve family and friends, and approach statutory agencies only after these people prove unable or unwilling to assist (Hanmer 1994). Each individual woman's situation is different but typically characterized by common features. One of these concerns the conditional support given by those the woman knows; another relates to the large number of voluntary (nonprofit) and statutory (state) agencies women must approach in order to receive assistance.

In a recent study of West Yorkshire, women approached on average ten agency types before receiving the help they needed (Hanmer 1994). This is not a measure of the number of visits to each agency or their multiple offices, but agency classifications, i.e., police, housing, social security, social services, hospitals, probation agencies, solicitors, and voluntary agencies to name a few. Such agencies can have a marginal impact on a woman's situation, or they can make it significantly worse or better. Women continue to approach agencies until some solution, however inadequate, is reached. In Britain, this often involves moving away from family and friends into an area where women and their children know no one. This alienating condition can prove a more serious hardship for those women with children living in greatest poverty. While the move may enhance a woman's physical safety, it limits her access to familiar social support, and financial hardship limits her ability to make new contacts: for example, there is no money for babysitters or bus fares.

Recent research into women's experiences of violence and agency responses also explores differences between women, particularly between women from Asian communities, with and without English language skills, and white women (Hanmer 1994) and amongst Black women (Mama 1989).[4] Both these studies show that the response of agencies is an important creator of differences in how women experience violence and its resolution. For example, Asian and Black women are more likely to be assisted by voluntary sector agencies and less likely to be assisted by statutory agencies, such as housing and social services. But, proportionally, Asian women are more likely to use the criminal justice system to resolve their problems than are white women (Hanmer 1994). There are other ways in which Asian and Black women are adversely affected. A woman's immigration status can make it much more difficult for a woman to successfully resolve a violent situation, particularly when she does not have an independent right to remain in Britain or cannot easily prove that right (e.g., her passport and other papers have been taken from her by the man and his family).

Although these are important differences, there are common themes whatever a woman's ethnic origin and background. If agencies and activists are to provide quality services to women who seek their assistance, an understanding of these commonalities is essential. One that continually surfaced in interviews is the importance of family for women. Regardless of marital status, ethnicity or culture, the first major commonality between women is that they live within a complex web of relationships. Family members and others play a pivotal role in women's lives. Second, women struggle against the domination, control, coercion and violence directed at them through

---

4. Black and Asian migrants and subsequent generations from Africa, Asia, the Caribbean, and other parts of the world form 7 percent of the total population of 55 million in Great Britain in 1991 (Office of Population Census and Surveys 1993). This is an urban population, primarily in England, with concentrations of specific ethnic groups in different parts of the country. The differential distribution of migrants was encouraged by specific industrial recruitment during the 1960s (e.g., Pakistanis to work in the woolen mills of West Yorkshire and immigrants from Barbados for the London Underground); later economic migrants and those forced to leave their home country as a result of political changes also settled where they knew others, e.g., Asians from Kenya in North London.

the web of relationships within which their lives are located. That is, women are not passive victims to whom unspeakable things happen. Women engage in a process of daily struggle to improve the quality of life for themselves and for those for whom they assume responsibility, usually, though not exclusively, their children. The term "survivor" does not adequately convey this condition. Thirdly, however diverse cultures may be in other ways, women exist within the interiors of their own cultures. The cultural boundaries that specify correct behavior for women are not those that bind men. This last and most basic factor constitutes the framework that either fully or partially legitimizes the violence men perpetrate against women in their homes. In individual situations, women recounted how, while some criticized their abuse, others helped support such behavior and even actively encouraged it. This raises the issue of what cultural boundaries are for men.

Women's attempts to resolve violence include personal struggles, the involvement of others, and distinctive cultural boundaries that differ for women and men. As women explain the details of their lives, the outstanding, overarching impression is that men are accountable neither to their community, family, nor statutory agencies. In the final analysis, despite possible objections, the reality is that men can place their affections, loyalties, income, and time elsewhere and still maintain their position as husband and father in the eyes of others. This behavior is impossible for women. Those who place their affections, loyalties, income, and time elsewhere are inevitably defined by others as bad wives and mothers against whom social sanctions must be introduced and enforced. Although not all women are equally affected, there is a clear double standard in operation that impacts on women regardless of their cultural group.

In all the cultural and ethnic groups from which women came in this British study, men have cultural and family advantages that come both from being male and from being husbands. This may, in part, explain why men are often loath to give up the women they abuse. In relinquishing "their women," they lose the gendered social advantages gained by being a husband and have only those of being male to fall back upon. When women establish themselves as single parents, men who are not immediately with another woman become single and itinerant, a lowly social position as men age. Affiliation with or control over a family carries considerable power and status for men in any community.

The British example merely illustrates social processes in one of the European Union member nations. Although the specifics of law and institutional processes vary, the broad outlines of women's situation is very similar. It is encapsulated in the reports, recommendations and actions taken by European-wide institutions.

European Initiatives and International Connections

The Council of Europe, an organization with a membership larger than the European Union, first adopted a Resolution on Violence in the Family in 1985 (26 March 1985). This included recommendations for action by Member States to further the prevention, official reporting, and state intervention when violence occurs. The Council of Europe continued its interest in violence against women with a Resolution on Social Measures (15 January 1990) and a further 1991 Solemn Declaration. These reports and resolutions follow the reasoning developed by women offering women-centered services to others—an approach further developed by feminist researchers.

In 1984, the Women's Rights Committee of the European Parliament began to consider violence against women and, in 1986, produced a parliamentary resolution and report (d'Ancona 1984; OJ C 176/73, 11 June 1986). This comprehensive report recognized the importance of refuges and changes in statutory agency responses. It further encouraged national legislation to achieve a more just response to women.[5]

Women increasingly mobilized within a more global arena to achieve regional improvements for women. In the mid-1980s women in Europe began to argue that the Universal Declaration of Human Rights also means women's rights (Ashworth 1986). The motion for the 1986 resolution to the European Parliament begins with a list of additional declarations, conventions, and resolutions that link human rights, civil and political rights, and the elimination of discrimination. These assertions and efforts continued during the next decade.[6] In preparation for the World Conference on Human Rights

5. The Report also includes additional resolutions submitted to the European Parliament. These are a call for action against sexual harassment and sexual blackmail in the workplace, sexual violence (including that committed against children), trafficking in women, prostitution and pornography. It also recommends the development of teaching methods on relations between women and men.

6. Specific conventions cited in the argument that human rights include women's rights are: (1) The Universal Declaration of Human Rights (1948); (2)

in June 1993, the world regional meetings in Africa, Latin America, and Asia also acknowledged that women universally are denied full citizenship rights (Ashworth 1993). Violence against women becomes one of many ways in which this occurs. This may seem logical in a country where the legal and constitutional systems are based on individual rights, but these rights are not necessarily the basis of national social orders around the world.

Part of the problem for women globally is the transfer of European state formations to other parts of the world through colonialism. While legal systems varied from country to country in Europe, the principle of male domination over women was incorporated in the different legal systems, for example, the British, Dutch, French, and Spanish. Citizenship was vested in men; the revolutions in France, and later in the United States, reinforced this position. Fraternity, liberty, and equality, the basic principles of these revolutions, defined a new relationship of men to the state. Women, however, continued to be subsumed under the legal guardianship of men. Without an independent legal identity, marriage could not be between equals. While the legal position of women in Europe has been modified, there is a negative legacy as a result of this earlier history. As Georgina Ashworth explains:

> this unbalanced consolidation of different persons into a domestic unit was taken up by the early economists and political theorists, and is responsible for the continued use today of the household as the unit of social and economic models, despite the culture of individualism, it is also still responsible for many of the implicit barriers to women's political participation and representation as a social group, and is a major factor in most women's experience of human rights (1993, 14–15).

The result is that men have the right to control women's time and property as well as their bodies. In the colonized world, the effect of the global proliferation of these Western political ideologies and

---

The International Covenant on Civil and Political Rights (ICCPR) 1966, in force 1976; (3) The International Covenant on Economic, Social, and Cultural Rights (ICESCR) 1966; (4) The Convention for the Elimination of all forms of Discrimination Against Women (CEDAW) 1979, in force 1981; (5) The Convention on the Rights of the Child (CRC) 1989; (6) The International Convention on the Elimination of All Forms of Racial Discrimination (ICERD) 1965; (7) The Convention Against Torture and Other Cruel, Inhuman, or Degrading Treatment or Punishment (CAT) 1984, in force 1987; (8) The Convention on the Right of Migrant Workers and Their Families, 1980.

practices undermined traditional law and social rules which gave women some control over their lives.

The Declaration on the Elimination of Violence Against Women was adopted by the General Assembly of the United Nations without a vote on 20 December 1993. This Declaration calls upon nation-states to undertake activities which eliminate violence against women. While there are no sanctions against countries which do not respond positively to this Declaration, it should be regarded as a result of women's world opinion and activism (United Nations 1993a; 1993b). Organizations, including world regional networks, continue to develop, and meetings such as the Fourth World Conference on Women provide rare opportunities for world discussions on and by women.[7]

The European Union countries and the wider European community held a regional meeting in preparation for the Fourth World Conference in which violence against women was on the agenda. Women are now working on local, national, world regional, and international levels to restrict the power of men to abuse women. All of this activity by many women comes from the early activism arising from the women's liberation movements of the West. The provision of appropriate services, that is, refuges for women and their children, remains the foundation upon which activism on violence against women in their homes from known men rests. While women are a very long way from achieving the elimination of such brutality, massive, although far from complete, strides in overcoming an organizational deficit at the international level are being made.

The European Context

For women in Europe, the European Union is perhaps the last governmental level that women moved to influence. That is because the European Union began as an economically driven treaty. Only issues directly concerned with economics were open for consideration. In the 1990s, this includes employment, unemployment, training, some aspects of education and science, technological research, and interstate cooperation to facilitate goods and services. A major

---

7. The Fourth World Conference on Women: Action for Equality, Development, and Peace was held in 1995 in Beijing. As well as the official governmental conference, it is estimated that 30,000 women attended the associated Forum meeting of non-governmental organizations (NGOs).

document under discussion is the Commission of the European Union White Paper on *Growth, Competitiveness, Employment* (European Commission 1994a). Although equal opportunities are mentioned occasionally, the issues of growth, competitiveness, and employment are largely discussed in "gender-neutral" language. The White Paper does not gender the implications of its strategies for women in relation to the labor market beyond suggesting that new jobs can be created from those tasks women now perform without pay (e.g., childcare and other caring activities). Issues pertaining to women in the family and the relationships between family members, welfare, and work remain largely unaddressed.

Only with the ratification of the Maastricht Treaty in 1993 did issues of social policy in a wider sense become a possible part of the European agenda for integration. The Green Paper on *European Social Policy: Options for the Union* explores the connection between social and economic policies (European Commission 1993a). However, the concern of this widely discussed document is with social exclusion, narrowly defined. Gendered differences are only recognized insofar as they relate to women's economic participation and the ways in which family responsibilities impact on this. For example, the report reveals that over a quarter of all women in the European Union are heads of households, living alone or as single parents; one half are in paid work at least part-time; women are having fewer children, 1.59, and at a later age, twenty-six years (European Commission 1993a, 24). These aspects of women's lives are mentioned because these are the elements of women's lives which buttress or deter capitalism's efficiency. Other issues that are believed to impinge less directly on this—issues like violence against women—are not recognized as relevant. The White Paper on *European Social Policy* (European Commission 1994), was issued after consultation with Member States on the Green Paper and incorporates key issues in the previously mentioned White Paper on *Growth, Competitiveness, Employment* (European Commission 1994a).

The White Paper on *Growth, Competitiveness, Employment* (European Commission 1994a) defines the strategic objective of the Union as moving from equal rights to equal treatment in the labor market. Equality of opportunity (for women) in society is encouraged only insofar as to better utilize women's experiences and skills for the benefit of society as a whole, including increased participation in the decision-making process (European Commission 1994, 25). Even though the European Commission recognizes that Europe is now faced with "unacceptable levels" of unemployment, inequality between women and men, poverty and social exclusion, and growing insecurity in the workplace, its approach misses completely the importance of violence against women in maintaining women's social subordination (European Commission 1994, 33). Rather, progress is to be attained through restoring growth and addressing the structural barriers to job creation (European Commission 1994, 36). Social integration is similarly regarded as the way to cope with a range of issues from third country nationals, to racism and xenophobia to urban-rural development. The White Paper on *European Social Policy* is equally myopic, although it contains a chapter on equality of opportunity for women and men with a subsection on reconciling employment and household and family life (1994, 41–45).

The European Union agenda is one that excludes most of women's lives, in particular, the complexity of the connections between family, work, welfare, and the labor market. Violence against women from known men can only be understood within this context. Integrating the relevance of violence against women into the conception of European integration involves dismantling the seamless way in which no space is allowed for raising the issue of violence against women in their homes. Just as women had, and have, to be inventive in finding ways to raise the issue of violence against women by known men at the national and international levels, so must they be at the European level. Breaking into the "gender neutral" economistic discourse of the European Union, whose key terms are harmonization, cohesion, federalism, subsidiarity, and transparency, can only be accomplished by gendering these core concepts. This process has begun with a recent report on the contribution of women's studies to European integration. It was presented to the Equality Unit in the European Commission (Hanmer et al. 1994). In gendering these key terms, major areas of concern to women, including violence from known men, can be included in the discourse of the European Union.

In this report, privatizing the power of men in families is presented as a barrier to social and economic integration (social cohesion) for women. The argument is that social discrimination is encouraged and maintained by unchecked violence against women. Violence against women is defined as a citizenship issue, whatever form it takes and wherever it occurs. With violence the state is involved in the denial of full citizenship rights to women through the selective ways state services are delivered to women and, less obviously, through the political divisions of public and private.

Defining women through their relationship to men in families for social and welfare entitlements, including that of physical safety, is the conceptual basis of private and public spheres in relation to women. Obtaining one's rights through men has the effect of ensuring women's social subordination. Given this system of social organization, it should come as no surprise that, in practice, women cannot obtain their formal rights to personal security that are promised in theory.

Raising the issues involved in violence against women within Europe will be as arduous as doing so on any other governmental level. Some initial suggestions are that this must include increased support for refuge movements and other women-directed services for women (e.g., rape crisis services and those to counter child sexual abuse). Strengthening the financial contribution to networks of national refuge movements and other women-centered services for Europeanwide meetings is essential for the successful development and implementation of pragmatic policies to counter violence against women. Ongoing involvement of women throughout the Union is necessary if efforts are to prove effective. At a time when European Union parliamentary processes are becoming more central, women need to develop close organizational links with the Women's Rights Committee and women Members of Parliament more generally. From this, a larger place within the European Commission and other European Union structures is needed for women-centered consultants, experts, and funded research. Such inclusion has helped women at the local and national levels and similar accomplishments need to be made at the European Union level. When considering violence, achieving equal treatment between women and men involves more than ensuring women and men have interchangeable roles and activities.

Conclusion

The European Union is the last governmental arena in which women have attempted to raise the issue of violence against women. The issue was first raised in individual countries and at the United Nations. There are several reasons for this: the EU is a relatively recent governmental entity, national governments place a greater emphasis on social policies than the European Union, and the United Nations through its Charter places a greater emphasis on human rights than the European Union, which is primarily an economic union. Raising violence against women in this political context involves expanding the theoretical location of the field known as violence against women to include citizenship, social and economic development, and overcoming pragmatic difficulties, such as access to decision makers and the under-funding of women's networks and projects. While this can be done, the analytic and pragmatic complexities of doing so should not be underestimated. However, our herstory of the past twenty years shows that, as long as women continue to be abused in their homes by the men with whom they live, other women will seek to assist and defend them. Women will find ways to gain social support to curtail the power of men. We live in hard times, but none of us should underestimate our own contributions and that of others in our demands for social justice for women.

10

THE EUROPEAN UNION AND THE FUTURE OF FEMINISM

Christine Delphy

The focus of this chapter is less on a unified Europe than on the future of feminism within it. For the purpose of brevity, I assert that, as elsewhere in the world, the future of feminism in Europe depends mostly on feminists themselves. The unification of Europe is, to my mind, less a problem than the unification of feminists on a clear definition of what a feminist approach is. This requires that two subjects be broached: First, how do we assess women's situation in the different countries that constitute Europe? That is, how do we solve the many problems associated with international comparisons? Second, how do we assess feminism in different countries, cultures, and political contexts? More to the point, what is feminism —what can and should it be? To what extent can it be a variable while still remaining an identifiable world-view shared by a global feminist community?

The future of feminism within Europe necessitates, first, some reflections on the notion of Europe as unified.

Toward a Unified Europe?

A unified Europe? To what extent can we speak of commonalities between nations when there is a vast cultural and linguistic heterogeneity within them? In other words, how can one address Europe as unified? At present, Europe is a political project not yet completed. Perhaps one can discuss this undertaking as "institutional Europe." But it remains questionable whether the societies and peoples of Europe have more in common than they had a few decades ago, when Europe was merely a geographical location. Any substantive generalizations about Europe as opposed to "institutional Europe" are, thus, unwarranted.

Even institutional Europe (i.e., political Europe) is in turmoil. Not long ago, *Le Monde* commented on the widening gulf between northern and southern Europe. The editors noted a Spain ridden with corruption, populist adventures in Italy, and nationalistic leanings in Greece. Wondering how frail the link was between the two regions, the editors asked whether the north will resist the temptation, after the addition of the Scandinavian states and Austria, to let go of the south entirely (*Le Monde*, 7 May 1994).

These regional divisions affect Europe's ability to advance feminism, for only a strong Europe could do so, if it wanted to sway its Member States in the right direction. These divisions also inhibit feminism's influence on European institutions, although so far the European record has been amazingly good. Europe, as an entity that is more than the sum of its parts, has created more progressive legislation than any of the Member States, or than all of them together. However, the capacity of the Member States to pay only ceremonious attention to European legislation, or ignore it entirely, reveals the limited degree of political integration among European states. Moreover, it is unlikely that the prospects for greater integration will improve in the future. For example, if the French were now to hold a new election, the Maastricht Treaty would not be ratified. The French are no exception; the mood throughout Member State constituencies is far from enthusiastic. There are many reasons for such Euro-pessimism, although primary among them is that European integration is a huge free market designed by and for business. Profoundly aware of this, many Europeans doubt that the Union's market will solve unemployment and, instead, fear that it may worsen the problem.

That feminism is differently developed in different European countries is indisputable. However, the geographical proximity and new institutional blanket now gathering the countries of Europe into a single group sometimes makes us drop our caution.

Not long ago, the European Commission commissioned a series of national reports concerning women's studies programs in Europe, the findings of which were then published in a Belgian feminist journal (*Les Cahiers du GRIF*). Very often the national reports contained similar phrases such as "women's studies are well developed." These assessments were provided without any agreed upon definition of what "well developed" means. Moreover, such phrases were employed to describe very different objective situations.

The low level of actual non-governmental communication between the peoples of Europe and the focusing of each country on its national issues holds true for feminists as well. This is not to say that there is no networking at all. But it occurs more often at a regional level within Europe, for instance between Scandinavian countries or between Mediterranean countries, although much less frequently among the latter.

In matters of social policy and feminist activism, Europe is clearly cut at least in two halves: feminist projects are far fewer in southern Europe—Italy, Greece, Spain, and France. There is also a relative lack of curiosity about other feminist movements. This is very much consistent with the lack of interest these countries have traditionally demonstrated in the outside world. In northern Europe, by contrast, feminists are eager for information about other feminist movements and are well versed in foreign languages, with the exception of the British and probably the Irish. The attitude of southern European feminists vis-à-vis languages and the "outside world" is more similar to that of their countrywomen and men than to that of northern feminists. There is little doubt that the development of feminism in the Netherlands, and in particular women's studies, is related to the fact that the Dutch women have a keen knowledge of English-speaking countries' literature and more generally keep abreast of developments in other Western countries. By contrast, French feminists, even scholars, with few exceptions, have less access to international literature. In this, French feminist scholars are very similar to their male counterparts in the humanities.

After a talk at which I had expanded on my pet thesis that "things are worse in France," another European hotly contested my presentation. In the course of argument, she insisted, "Well, for example, when a woman goes to a rape crisis center ..." "What rape crisis center," I retorted. "I don't know, any, the one in Paris for example," said she. I could tell that she thought that I was stalling. "There is no rape crisis center in Paris," I answered. "Well, then in Lyon or Marseille," she continued assuming I was stalling even more. "There are no rape crisis centers there either," I said patiently. It took us ten minutes to disentangle what was not, strictly speaking, a misunderstanding, but rather a difficulty on her part to hear what I was saying. There was not and never had been one rape crisis center in France. She took for granted that if one has a feminist movement, or even the remains of one, one has a rape crisis center. She was unaware that she was making such an assumption or, rather, that it was an assumption.

When I retold the story to a French friend, she said: "but we do have a rape-line," to which I answered: "yes, but not a center, a place where you actually see people in the flesh." She admitted that what I said was true, but she did not seem particularly shocked by it, or envious of countries which do have centers; she did not seem to grasp the implications of the differences between a hot-line and an actual center. This suggests how easy it is to do without something that one never had in the first place.

If I were to embrace cultural relativism, I would assert that a hot-line is exactly what is attuned to the needs of French women and that we have no use for a real center. But on the contrary, I think we could use a center. If we do not have one, whereas the British have many of them, that is significant information for a comparison of the relative strengths of the two feminist movements. The presence of rape crisis centers and other such places testifies to the strength of a movement. The lack of even one such center both testifies to the weakness of the French movement and is a consequence of that weakness. Being fully aware of that condition explains my French friend's reaction. It is not that she does not know that a center is better than a hot-line and ten centers better than one, just as one is better than nothing; it is that she is resigned to France always lagging behind in feminist respects. She shows a lot of sophistication, which is, itself, the result of international activism. Yet, many feminists, for lack of information and points of comparison, are unable to assess their country's stage of advancement in feminist achievements. This is very often the case in France, but I suspect it is also the case in other European countries.

European countries are neither so unified nor homogeneous. The realization that some countries are more or less sexist than others is necessary but insufficient for assessing feminism in Europe and the conditions for women in the different countries that comprise it. There remains a serious quandary for those involved in comparing European nations according to women's status—one must find the instruments for making comparisons while demonstrating an analytical aptitude to discern the problems involved in making them.

Assessing Women's Conditions

Inasmuch as there is a striving towards theoretical sophistication, and complex models of women's subordination being evolved at the theoretical level, when it comes to descriptions and/or inter-European or international comparisons, we tend to use unthinkingly the rate of employment as not only an indicator, but the major one for ascertaining women's overall status. For instance, scholars usually describe French women's rate of employment as "high" and Dutch women's rate of employment as "low." However, even though it is not said, the points of comparison are not men's rates of employment nor women's rates of employment worldwide.

The terms "high" or "low" implicitly refer to the European average rate, and within Europe, these two rates can be deemed to constitute two poles. But, if one takes a wider point of view, the differences between these two rates of employment do not seem all that significant—they certainly do not represent extreme situations, or opposed models. In France and the Netherlands, at most two-thirds of all women are full-time housewives. In both countries, at most half of all women are engaged in paid work. The reasons why a difference which involves a quarter of the population is deemed so important are never made clear. However, to insist that this difference is significant, one would have to make the hypothesis that this difference between full-time housewives and working women affects women's status more generally. Most importantly, writing that the level of women's employment is "high" or "low" implies an idea of what the normal level of employment among women is or should be.

If we are confronted with problems when interpreting facts, what about the problems we meet when the nature of the "fact" itself, not to mention its measurement, becomes elusive?

How can we compare sexual harassment in different countries, the laws, when they exist, concerning it, and its occurrence? Sexual harassment as a term is an import from English to French. This is true in other languages as well. People do not readily understand what it means. Yet, this terminology was chosen because feminists in France, as well as those at the European Commission, wanted to call attention to a whole set of attitudes and behaviors that previously had no name. They wished to establish legal remedies that could mitigate the harms associated with the behaviors.

In 1991, the European Commission passed a Recommendation and a Code of Practice against sexual harassment. France was then the first country to legislate against it. But, although the French law was labeled in the media as the "Law Against Sexual Harassment," the bill does not use that wording. Indeed, French legislators have refused not only the wording but the whole conceptualization that the very phrase encapsulates.

The French law is, in many respects, unrecognizable to the very U.S. and European legislators who originally conceived sexual harassment as a behavior to be legislated against. The French law is specifically directed only against the "abuse of authority to obtain favors of a sexual nature." To argue that the French adopted a core element of the American and Commission approach is entirely misleading.

It is not that the French are reluctant to adopt what they see as a U.S. invention, although anti-Americanism was marshaled to oppose a feminist interpretation. Rather, the French manifest a genuine inability to understand what is encapsulated in the wording of the European recommendation. After all, the Commission deems reprehensible "any behavior based on sex which affects the dignity of women or men." It does not say: "Behavior of a sexual nature" but "Behavior based on sex." What transpires in this short sentence is an understanding that sexual acts may not be the only, or even the ultimate, goal of sexual harassment. Instead, sexuality in all its guises may be used for the wider, more long-term aim of affirming gender domination by gender humiliation. It is this awareness of gender domination, and the decision to outlaw it, which is at the core of the U.S. legislation and European recommendation. By contrast, gender domination is recognized by neither the French state nor the wider French political class.[1]

Even after it was politically weakened, the French bill came as a shock to male public opinion. While men insisted that the bill would create problems between the sexes where previously there existed none, they were not alone in that perception. As is often the case, public opinion polls pertaining to sexual harassment were taken before the bill was introduced. Of all the examples provided, only the most blatant cases of sexual blackmail evoked the response that the behavior was sexual harassment by more than half the respondents. In most other examples of sexual harassment, a majority of those polled were reluctant to classify the behavior as such. One of the most revealing examples included a young woman being whistled at in the street. When asked whether this constituted sexual harassment, 82 percent of men and 84 percent of women answered no (*Le Point*, 25 January 1992).

Sexual harassment is behavior of a sexual nature, or more generally, between the sexes as genders, that is deemed reprehensible. By distinguishing discourteous, sexist annoyances from sexual

1. This political class includes, but is not reduced to, opinion makers, the media, and publicized intellectuals.

harassment, the French suggest that they think that it is legitimate for men to treat women in this manner. That women's answers generally resemble those of men does not suggest that they, the victims of harassment, are not affected by it. They are affected. Their answers suggest that, although sexual harassment may perturb them, they regard the behavior as a male right. It is, however, unlikely that women would state this so explicitly, although the French media have been quite lyrical about this "right." The crux of their argument is that sexual harassment is part of a sexual continuum and that, although some parts of sexuality may be painful, the alternative is to do without any sexual encounters at all.

In France, gendered behavior is sexualized, passed as sex, and sex is good. Feminists in France exploded that myth as regards rape in 1976 and 1977 when we promoted the analysis: sex is sex and rape is violence. Met with a backlash which served to debilitate us, we never got to explore the more radical feminist tenet that violence is male sexuality (MacKinnon 1987; 1989). While this analysis may not be stated so expressly within a U.S. and European legislative context, the analysis underpins it. It is an analysis that explores not only sexual violence, but suggests that sexuality itself is a way to maintain a gendered hierarchy. This awareness informed neither the French bill nor the content of discourse pertaining to it. Nonetheless, the analysis is present in the minds of young working French women who know that sexual harassment is not confined to attempts to achieve sexual access.

Interviews I have conducted with female train controllers, who work in all-male environments, show that they rarely regard the sexual harassment to which they are subjected (often in the form of lewd jokes) as having anything to do with "obtaining sexual favors." On the contrary, the women are quite definite that when a man is really interested in a woman in that environment, he refrains from such behavior. The men know, and the women know, that this bantering not only will not lead to a sexual encounter but will stand in its way. Yet, the women do not have an analysis to express what it is that this taunting is designed to accomplish. Namely, sexual harassers are attempting to elicit an acceptance of male dominance from the women who work with them and evoke resignations from those who refuse to comply.

If we compare public opinion polls, how are we to understand the figures showing that 40 percent of women in the United States have been subjected to sexual harassment, as against 20 percent of French women? How are we to make comparisons when we may not be speaking to the same issues and events? How will we compare figures about court cases, which will undoubtedly inscribe the cases brought under the French law as "sexual harassment"?

Such questions lead to the problem raised by figures on crimes against women: do high figures mean high occurrences and low figures low occurrences? Or, do such figures suggest exactly the reverse: do low figures on incest, prior to feminist campaigning, suggest that this crime was silenced? This classic problem for feminists is only compounded when we are doing international research, which European research is. If one country has higher rape figures than another, does it mean that women are more subjected to violence in the first or that conditions for reporting rape are worse in the second? Research concerning incest and child-molesting suggests that lower figures are disquieting because they may indicate under-reporting.

Another problem in international comparison is the tendency to rely on laws as indicators of women's status. This implies that laws that have the same labels in different countries cover the same phenomena. The French law on sexual harassment demonstrates clearly that this is not the case. Moreover, to imply that all laws are enforced in the same way in all countries or that all laws are enforced the same way in any single country is a problem. For example, the Spanish and French laws pertaining to abortion appear strikingly similar in that they permit abortions until ten weeks after conception. But the massive use of the "conscious clause" by Spanish doctors who refuse to perform legal hospital abortions makes a mockery of the law.

To focus exclusively on legal texts is to ignore their pragmatic consequences. In addition, France's law is being eroded by a host of factors. For example, state-run clinics are often so overcrowded that many women are unable to meet the ten-week stipulation. Still, more doctors refuse to perform this medical procedure. Such conditions explain why 5,000 French women went to the Netherlands to get abortions in 1992 (*CADAC Newsletter* 1993). Although the Netherlands has a repressive abortion law on their books, it is not enforced. Consequently, the Dutch practice of abortion is more liberal than in many countries that have legalized the practice. These circumstances demonstrate that women's situation not only depends on favorable laws being enforced; it depends also on repressive laws not being enforced or not existing. Ideally, no laws should be required to overcome the reluctance of medical professionals and society at large to regard abortion as any other surgical intervention. When women need permission for this procedure, the law maintains abortion as a special practice, the legitimacy of which can always be questioned.

In short, laws that appear to be favorable to women (e.g., the French and Spanish laws) do not reveal information concerning their practical consequences. Indeed, Dutch policies reveal the extent to which laws can be constructed and ignored. More importantly, laws specifically designed to uphold women's rights (to abortion) may suggest that women are in such serious jeopardy from societal resistance that they need legal protection. As the nineteenth-century French author Lacordiare wrote: "Between the strong and the weak, the rich and the poor, the master and the servant, it is freedom which oppresses and law which liberates."

Charting lists of laws affecting women in different countries for the purpose of assessing women's relative situations may give a quite erroneous view of how countries compare. And comparing notes is the stuff of which feminist meetings are made.

Feminism: Variable and World-View

Whether we want to assess women's situation or the state of feminism, the same problems arise. First, a description always implies comparison, and comparisons are always value-laden (e.g., "women are worse off here, better off there" and "women's studies are underdeveloped here as compared to there"). This is inescapable. The answer is not to decree that we stop comparing or that we try attaining value-free assessments. Such goals are unrealistic. Any description implies comparison. No country or phenomenon can be described in isolation. Second, there are things that are either immeasurable or not yet measured. One such indicator is the level of "feminism" (or "sexism") in a country.

Cultural relativism is so often raised against feminism that now it is even called for from within it. Lois West published an article in *Women's Studies International Forum* entitled "Feminist National Social Movements: Beyond Universalism and Towards a Gendered Cultural Relativism." In it, she insists that there are "cultural differences in interpretation and definition over the meaning of feminism which are not simply questions of semantics but of profoundly differing world-views" (West 1992, 576). Indeed. However, we need not call all world-views feminist, even if they are uttered by women. After all, not all women are feminist. Furthermore, feminism may have no meaning at all if it can accommodate profoundly different world-views. If feminism is not a world-view, and I think it should be, it becomes just another term for women or women's interests. This means little, especially as these interests can be defined so differently.

A lot of "cultural specificity" talk has been brought to bear on the debate about sexual harassment in France. As the concept is deemed, not unfairly, to have come from the United States, it has sparked a lot of anti-Americanism; and vice versa, anti-Americanism, which is a container common to many different ideologies, has been called on to rescue French mores.

It has been alleged that the problem of sexual harassment did not exist in France. France has been deemed a haven of gentility, a "special place where the sexes love each other." The opponents of the law, or of the United States, have tried to proffer an image of France as the only nation where the sexes are not at war and actually make love. Of course, no one is really so naive as to believe this. The irrational nature of the argument is revealed fully when we hear its proponents explain that the "mildness of the French climate" might be responsible for that wonderful state of affairs. Intentional or not, France as an oasis of gentleness in a world of brutes is a recurring French self-image that is mostly applied to the relations between women and men, although not solely.

French whimpering about their "cultural exceptionalism" is as wearying as cultural relativism. One is no more valid than the other. As one of my anthropology professors told us long ago, when talking about the Ancient Incas: respecting cultures does not mean being ignorant; ripping out the heart from a live person is cruel. Some cultures are more sexist than others, just as some are more cruel. Customs do not have or should not have a lease on eternal life just because they exist. In their attempts to change their respective societies from within, feminists trample on the foot of old customs. Even if we value our past and our traditions, we are ready to sacrifice them for what we deem higher values, such as the dignity of human beings.

All societies change. They are never eternal. Many anthropologists have convinced us that some societies are "cold," do not change and dare outside history. Such characterizations are part of the Western myth, or longing, which, with the help of racism, has been projected on so-called primitive societies. But, it is patronizing to think that some societies do not change, cannot and should not change. Furthermore, it is a naive, albeit widely shared, view of social change. According to that view, change requires action, whereas non-change requires only the force of inertia. This is erroneous. Not changing requires as much energy as changing. To take but one example: in the last decade a gendered division of labor was invented where none existed before because neither the tools (e.g., the computers) nor the skills existed before. Throughout the West, the gendered dimensions of brand-new computer technologies could not have happened through inertia. On the contrary, inertia would have produced a blurring, or rather a nonexistence of the gender-line; reproducing traditional social hierarchy in an entirely new technical setting has required a lot of imagination and energy. Conservation is an action.

In any given place, at any given time, what we note as the social structure and its attendant culture is the result of the power struggle between different forces at work within a particular society. That balance is always precarious. French feminists do not endorse or believe in the rhetoric of the French exception. They regard it for what it is: a conservative line which appeals to the worst in people— their nationalistic tendencies. If, as Lois West argues, women can be feminist while opposing the notion of individual rights, abortion, or a public role for women—what is it that they support? Stated simply, they support those collective values that place the "collective good of the family and the nation first" (West 1992, 566-567). Having no definition of the "collective good" is cause for concern. Too often "communal values" conceal the individual interests of leaders, irrespective of the group's size. As well, the "good of the family" has, for centuries, been a code word for promoting the interests of Western husbands and fathers. Lois West tries to convince us that bona fide feminists throughout the world, from the Philippines to Northern Ireland, share the same nationalistic goals and pro-family views of their male counterparts. There is no question that many women share the perspectives of men, but to do this is not feminist.

In 1991, the Algerian government preempted women's constitutional right to vote by allowing vote by proxy. A man could have as many as five proxies. All that was required was that he show the passports of his wife and adult children or other family members. Algerian *feminists* waged a campaign against what they saw as a distortion of the constitution and an attack on democracy. After a long battle, the constitutional court had to side with them. These women did not try to undermine their country. They simply do not believe that the rights of women, or any other individuals, have to be sacrificed on the altar of the collective good. Although Algerian men may insist that these women have been unduly influenced by Western feminists and foreign values, Algerian feminists are clear that any "collective good" that would require them to sacrifice their rights is a community predicated upon a definition of the nation as all-male.

Let us be clear. The so-called opposition between selfish feminist individualism and generous collective nationalism requires that we ask which individual interests are combined to constitute the collective good. In asking that question, we note that there are not that many different ways of being feminist. Yet, because it has become fashionable in some parts to be a self-proclaimed feminist, some women have chosen to define the "collective good" in male terms. Promoting male interests (or even failing to challenge them) does not entitle women to respect as feminists.

Conclusion

We do not need feminism to be adopted by all and sundry: there is no percentage in it for us. Being female is not synonymous with being feminist. Feminism is a progressive ideology which (at this point in time) cannot be shared by all, inasmuch as we would like this to be the case. It is disquieting when everybody claims to be a feminist when we know it cannot be true.

We do not need to enlarge feminism so that it can accommodate everyone. It is to our detriment to adopt a wider, more vague and "anything goes" definition of feminism. Instead, we need to define more precisely what we mean, so that we can lead coherent, coordinated and efficient actions in our own countries and internationally. We need a narrower, more precise, more offensive, definition—perhaps we need fewer and better feminists.

REFERENCES

Angeles, Leonora C., and the Philippine Organizing Team. 1993. Between the Devil and the Deep Blue Sea: Transnational Issues and Trends in Trafficking of Filipino Women. In *Women Empowering Women: Proceedings of the Human Rights Conference on the Trafficking of Asian Women, 2–4 April,* 25–55. Metro Manila: Coalition Against Trafficking in Women, Asia-Pacific.

Ashworth, Georgina. 1986. *Of Violence and Violation: Women and Human Rights.* London: Change: International Reports: Women and Society (P.O. Box 824, London SE 24 9JX).

———. 1993. *Changing The disCourse: A Guide to Women and Human Rights.* London: Change: International Reports: Women and Society (P.O. Box 824, London SE 24 9JX).

AVFT. 1990. *De l'Abus de Pouvoir Sexuel: Le harcèlement sexuel au travail.* Paris: La Découverte.

Baer, Susanne, and Vera Slupik. 1988. Entwurf eines Gesetzes gegen Pornografie. *Kritische Justiz* 21 (2): 171–181.

Baer, Susanne. 1994. State, Law, and Women in Germany. In *Test the West: Gender Democracy and Violence,* 63–69. Vienna: Austrian Federal Ministry of Women's Affairs and the Federal Chancellery.

Banks, Karen. 1991. Equal Pay and Equal Treatment for Women and Men in Community Law. *Social Europe* 3. European Commission: 62–76.

Barry, Ursula. 1992. Movement, Change and Reaction: The Struggle over Reproductive Rights in Ireland. In *The Abortion Papers: Ireland,* ed. Ailbhe Smyth, 107–118. Dublin: Attic Press.

Baxter, Mike. 1990. Flesh and Blood: Does Pornography Lead to Sexual Violence? *New Scientist,* 5 May: 37–41.

Beattie, V. L. 1992. Analysis of the Results of a Survey on Sexual Violence in the UK, Paper presented to Cambridge Women's Forum. Cambridge: University Students Union.

Bindman, Geoffrey. 1992. Incitement to Racial Hatred in the United Kingdom: Have We Got the Law We Need? In *Striking a Balance: Hate Speech, Freedom of Expression and Non-Discrimination,* 258–262. London: Article 19.

Bowman, Cynthia G. 1993. Street Harassment and the Informal Ghettoization of Women. *Harvard Law Review* 106: 517–580.

Braidotti, Rosi. 1991. *Patterns of Dissonance.* Cambridge: Polity Press.

Brenner, Johanna. 1993. US Feminism in the Nineties. *New Left Review* (200): 101–159.

Briere, John, and Marsha Runtz. 1989. University Males' Sexual Interest in Children: Predicting Potential Indices of "Pedophilia" in a Non-forensic Sample. *Child Abuse and Neglect* 13: 65–75.

Broadcasting Standards Council. 1993. *Annual Report 1992–1993.* London: BSC.

Brodie, Janine, Shelly Gaqvigan, and Jane Jenson. 1992. *The Politics of Abortion.* Toronto: Oxford University Press.

Brussa, Lucia. 1991. Survey on Prostitution, Migration and Traffic in Women: History and Current Situation. Paper presented to Seminar on Action Against Traffic in Women, 25–27 September. Strasbourg: Council of Europe. EG/PROST (91).

Buckley, Mary, and Malcolm Anderson, eds. 1988. *Women, Equality and Europe.* London: Macmillan.

CADAC (Coordination nationale des Associations pour le Droit à l'Avortement et à la Contraception) Newsletter. 1993.

Cameron, David R. 1992. The 1992 Initiative: Causes and Consequences. In *Euro-Politics: Institutions and Policymaking in the "New" European Community,* ed. Alberta M. Sbragia, 23–74. Washington, D.C.: The Brookings Institute.

Carter, Victoria A. 1992. Working on Dignity: EC Initiatives on Sexual Harassment in the Work Place. *Northwestern Journal of International Law and Business* 12: 431–460.

Chan, Ying Chan. 1993. China Ships' Unholy Cargo. *Daily News,* 18 May.

Clapham, Andrew. 1991. *Human Rights in the European Community: A Critical Overview.* Baden-Baden: Nomos Press.

———. 1993. *Human Rights in the Private Sphere.* New York: Oxford University Press.

Clarity, James E. 1995. Ireland's Senate Debates Information on Abortion. *New York Times,* 13 March.

Coalition Against Trafficking in Women. 1993. A Tour of Olongapo, Subic Bay, Angeles. *Coalition Report.* P.O. Box 9338, North Amherst, Massachusetts 010589: 1–2.

Cockburn, Cynthia. 1994. *Women in the Europeanizing of Industrial Relations—A Study in Five Member States.* Brussels: European Commission: V/664/94.

Coenen, Marie-Thérèse. 1991. *La grève des femmes de la F.N. en 1966.* Brussels: Pol-His.

Cohen, Nick 1989. Reaping Rich Revenue from the Profit of Pornography. *Independent,* 18 December.

———. 1989. Impact of Images May Provoke Abuse. *Independent,* 19 December.

Coleman, Francis, and Sheena McMurtrie. 1993. Too Hot to Handle. *New Law Journal,* 8 January: 10–11.

Collins, Evelyn. 1991. The Implementation and Development of Community Equality Law. *Social Europe* 3. European Commission: 33–41.

Collins, Patricia Hill. 1993. Pornography and Black Women's Bodies. In *Making Violence Sexy: Feminist Views on Pornography,* ed. Diana E. H. Russell, 97–105. Milton Keynes: Open University Press.

Connell, Desmond. 1994. *The Irish Times,* 25 May.

Connelly, Alpha, ed. 1993. *Gender and the Law in Ireland.* Dublin: Oak Tree Press.

Conroy Jackson, Pauline. 1992. Twenty Years in the European Community. What Now? Boom or Doom. Address to 12th Pearse School, 10–11 April.

Corcoran, Clodagh. 1989. *Pornography: The New Terrorism.* Dublin: Attic Press.

Coughlan, Dennis. 1994. Divorce Referendum Plans on Hold until All Uncertainty Removed. *The Irish Times,* 29 May.

Council of Europe. 1993. *Strategies for the Elimination of Violence Against Women in Society: Media and Other Means,* Memorandum presented to the Swiss Delegation to the Third European Ministerial Conference on Equality Between Women and Men, 21–22 October, in Rome. Strasbourg: Council of Europe.

Cowe, Richard. 1993. Paul Raymond Still Headlines the Riches Revue. *Independent,* 15 September.

Cowell, Allan. 1993. "Natasha Syndrome" Brings on a Fever in Turkey. *New York Times*, 17 April.

Cumberbatch, Guy, and Dennis Howitt. 1989. *A Measure of Uncertainty: The Effects of the Mass Media*. Broadcasting Standards Council Research Monograph London: John Libbey.

d'Ancona, Hedy. 1984. *Report Drawn Up On Behalf of the Committee on Women's Rights on Violence Against Women*, European Parliament Reports, Luxembourg: Office for Official Publications of the European Communities.

Dane, Eva, and Renate Schmidt, eds. 1990. *Frauen & Männer und Pornographie*. Frankfurt: Fischer.

de Dios, Aurora Javate. 1993. The Global Trafficking in Asian Women. In *Women Empowering Women: Proceedings of the Human Rights Conference on the Trafficking of Asian Women, 2–4 April*, 3–10. Metro Manila, Philippines: Coalition Against Trafficking in Women, Asia-Pacific.

Delphy, Christine. 1993. Avertissement aux malfaisants—L'Avortement encore en cause. *Nouvelles Questions Féministes* 13 (4): 1–8.

Department of Justice. 1986. *Attorney General's Commission on Pornography*. Final Report, Washington, DC.

de Vires, Ineke. 1993. Informal Methods of Resolving Problems. Unpublished conference paper. Industrial Relations Services. June.

Dobash, R. Emerson, and Russell P. Dobash. 1979. *Violence Against Wives*. New York: The Free Press.

Docksey, C. 1987. The European Community and the Promotion of Equality. In *Women, Employment and European Equality Law*, ed. Christopher McCrudden, 1–22. London: Eclipse Publications.

Duchen, Claire. 1986. *Feminism in France From May 1968 to Mitterrand*. London: Routledge & Kegan Paul.

Dworkin, Andrea, and Catharine A. MacKinnon. 1988. *Pornography and Civil Rights*. Minneapolis: Organizing Against Pornography.

Dworkin, Ronald. 1985. *A Matter of Principle*. Cambridge, Massachusetts: Harvard University Press.

Easton, Susan. 1994. *The Problem of Pornography: Regulation and the Right to Free Speech*. London: Routledge.

Edwards, Susan. 1992. Pornography: A Plea for Law Reform. *Denning Law Journal*: 41–64.

Ellis, Evelyn. 1991. *European Community Sex Equality Law*. Oxford: Oxford University Press.

Elman, R. Amy, and Maud L. Eduards. Unprotected by the Swedish Welfare State: A Survey of Battered Women and the Assistance They Received. *Women's Studies International Forum* 14 (5): 413–421.

Emelda, Albertina. 1988. Tourism as a Method of Exploitation for Prostitution both Nationally and Internationally. In *Exploitation of Women and Children: Its Causes and Effects*, 142–145. Report of Asian Regional Conference, organized by the International Abolitionist Federation in collaboration with Association for Social Health in India, Joint Women's Programme, and Indian Health Organization, 17–19 November. New Delhi, India.

Equal Opportunities Commission. 1993. *Women and Men in Britain 1993*. London: HMSO.

Euripides I. 1944. Translated and edited by Rex Warner. London: The Bodley Head Limited.

European Commission. 1993. *How to Combat Sexual Harassment at Work: A Guide to Implementing the EC Code*. Brussels: Office for Official Publications of the European Communities.

———. 1993a. *European Social Policy*, Green Paper, COM (93) 551, 17 November.

———. 1994. *European Social Policy: A Way Forward for the Union*, White Paper, COM (94) 333, 27 July.

———. 1994a. *Growth, Competitiveness, Employment: The Challenges and Way Forward into the 21st Century*, White Paper, COM (93) 700 Final.

European Industrial Relations Review. 1992. Legislation on Sexual Harassment. 227: 12–13.

European Women's Lobby. 1995. *Confronting the Fortress—Black and Migrant Women in the European Community*. Luxembourg: European Parliament.

Financial Times. 1995. EMU Strain Begins to Show, 17 January.

Firestone, Shulamith. 1971. *The Dialectic of Sex*. London: Paladin.

Fiss, Owen M. 1976. Groups and the Equal Protection Clause. *Philosophy & Public Affairs* 5 (2): 107–177.

Fletcher, George P. 1993. Constitutional Identity. *Cardozo Law Review* 14 (3–4): 737–757.

Fletcher, Ruth. 1993. The Significance of Irish Women's Silence about their Experiences of Abortion. Master's Thesis, University College Cork.

Forna, Aminatta. 1992. Pornography and Racism: Sexualising Violence and Inciting Hatred. In *Pornography: Women, Violence and Civil Liberties*, ed. Catherine Itzin, 102–113. Oxford: Oxford University Press.

Franklin, Sarah. 1991. Fetal Fascinations: New Dimensions to the Medical-Scientific Construction of Fetal Personhood. In *Off-Centre: Feminism and Cultural Studies*, ed. S. Franklin, C. Lury, and J. Stacey, 190–205. London: Harper Collins.

Fraser Commission. 1985. *Report of the Special Committee on Pornography and Prostitution*, Pornography and Prostitution in Canada. Ottawa.

Fredman, Sandra. 1992. European Community Discrimination Law: A Critique. *Industrial Law Journal* 21 (2): 119–134.

French, Howard W. 1992. For the World's Brothels, Caribbean Daughters. *New York Times*, 20 April.

Gambardello, Joseph A. 1993. International Sex Slave Free: Korean "Fugitives" Nabbed. *New York Newsday*, 1 May.

Gay, Jill. 1985. Asian Governments Pander to Tourists. *New York Newsday*, 7 June.

Gladwell, Malcolm, and Rachel E. Stassen-Berger. 1993. Human Cargo is Hugely Profitable to New York's Chinese Underworld. *The Washington Post*, 7 June.

Glendon, Mary Ann. 1991. *Rights Talk: The Impoverishment of Political Discourse*. New York Free Press.

Goggin, Malcolm L., ed. 1993. *Understanding the New Politics of Abortion*. London: Sage.

Gupta, Jyotsna Agnihotri. 1991. Women's Bodies: The Site for the Ongoing conquest by Reproductive Technologies. *Issues in Reproductive and Genetic Engineering* 4 (2): 93–107.

Hagman, Ninni. 1992. *Measures Taken in Sweden to Combat Sexual Harassment at Work*. Geneva: Report to the International Labour Office (ILO).

Hall, Ruth. 1985. *Ask Any Woman*. Bristol: Falling Wall Press.

Hanmer, Jalna. 1982. Reprint. Violence and Social Control of Women. *Feminist Issues*, 2 (1): 53–74. Original edition, in *Power and the State*, ed. Gary Littlejohn,

Barry Smart, John Wakeford and Nina Yuval-Davis, 217–238. London: Croom Helm, 1978.

_____, and Sheila Saunders. 1984. *Well-Founded Fear: A Community Study of Violence to Women*. London: Hutchinson.

_____, and Sheila Saunders. 1993. *Women, Violence and Crime Prevention*. Aldershot: Gower.

_____. 1994. *Policy Development and Implementation Seminars: Patterns of Agency Contact with Women*, Research Paper No. 12, Violence, Abuse and Gender Relations Research Unit, University of Bradford, U.K.

_____, Rosi Braidotti, Dearbhal Ni Chartaigh, Johanna Kootz, Liliane Kandel, Mary Nash, and Birgit Petersson. 1994. *Women's Studies and European Integration: With reference to current and future Action Programmes for Equal Opportunities between Women and Men*, Report to the Equal Opportunities Unit. Brussels: Commission of the European Communities.

Harris, Louis. 1991. *Le Harcèlement Sexuel: Enquête des Français, Perceptions, Opinions et Evaluation du Phénomène*. Paris, December.

Hegarty, Trish. 1994. Medical Council Member Calls for Openness. *The Irish Times*, 30 April.

Hoff, Joan. 1994. Comparative Analysis of Abortion in Ireland, Poland and the USA. *Women's Studies International Forum* 17 (6): 621–646.

Hoigard, Cecile, and Liv Finstad. 1992. *Backstreets: Prostitution, Money, and Love*. Cambridge: Polity Press.

Home Office Criminal Statistics 1985–1989. London: HMSO.

Hoskyns, Catherine. 1985. Women's Equality and the European Community. *Feminist Review* 20: 71–88.

_____. 1992. The European Community's Policy on Women in the Context of 1992. *Women's Studies International Forum* 15 (1): 21–28.

Howitt, Dennis, and Guy Cumberbatch. 1990. *Pornography: Impacts and Influences*. Research and Planning Unit. London: Home Office.

Hubert, Florence C. 1994. *Enforcement of the EC Discrimination Law in France*. Internal Report. Paris: Secrétaire des droits des femmes.

ICPO-INTERPOL. 1988. *Exploitation of Women and Children: Its Causes and Effects*. Report of Asian Regional Conference, organized by the International Abolitionist Federation in collaboration with Association for Social Health in India, Joint Women's Programme, and Indian Health Organization, 17–19 November. New Delhi, India.

Inglis, Tom. 1987. *Moral Monopoly: The Catholic Church in Modern Irish Society*. Dublin: Gill and Macmillan.

International Labour Office (ILO) 1992. *Combating Sexual Harassment at Work*. Geneva: ILO.

Itzin, Catherine, and Rachel Wingfield. 1992. *Pornography: Visible Harm?*, Channel 4 Dispatches Factsheet, November.

Itzin, Catherine. 1992. *Pornography: Women, Violence and Civil Liberties*. Oxford: Oxford University Press.

_____. 1994. *Pornography-Related Harm: A Review of the Evidence*. Report to the Home Office 1991, University of Bradford Violence and Abuse Unit Research Publication.

Jenson, Jane. 1989. Ce n'est pas un hasard: the Varieties of French Feminism. In *Contemporary France*, ed. Jolyon Holyworth and George Ross, 114–143. London: Frances Pinter.

Kappeler, Susanne. 1986. *The Pornography of Representation*. Cambridge: Polity Press.

_____. 1992 Pornography: The Representation of Power. In *Pornography: Women, Violence and Civil Liberties*, ed. Catherine Itzin, 88–102. Oxford: Oxford University Press.

Katzenstein, Mary, and Carol Mueller, eds. 1987. *The Women's Movements of the United States and Western Europe: Consciousness, Political Opportunity and Public Policy*. Philadelphia: Temple University Press.

Kelly, Liz, and Maureen O'Hara. 1990. The Making of Pornography: An Act of Sexual Violence. *Spare Rib* (203): 16–19.

Kingdon, John. 1984. *Agendas, Alternatives and Public Policies*. Boston: Little Brown.

Klein, Renate D. 1989. *Infertility: Women Speak Out about their Experience of Reproductive Medicine*. London: Pandora Press.

Kleinfield, N. R. 1995. Five Charged with Holding Thai Women Captive for Prostitution. *The New York Times*, 5 January.

Kofman, Eleonore, and Rosemary Sales. 1992. Toward Fortress Europe? *Women's Studies International Forum* 15 (1): 29–39.

Kvinnofronten. 1993. *Kvinnokunskap om EG/EU—makt, arbete och omsorg*. En debattskrift från Kvinnofronten. Spånga, Sweden: Kvinnofronten.

Labour Research. 1992. Standing Up to Sexual Harassment. May: 17–18.

Le Monde. 1994. Editorial Statement, 7 May.

Le Nouvel Observateur. 1989. Le Retour du Droit de Cuissage, 2–8 March.

Le Point. 1992. Sondage Ipsos/Le Point, 25 January, No. 1010.

Lester, T. 1993. The EEC Code of Conduct—Sexual Harassment. *New Law Journal*, 22 October: 1473–1474.

_____. 1993. The EEC Code of Conduct—Sexual Harassment. *New Law Journal*, 29 October: 1540–1541.

Lindemann, Barbara, and David D. Kadue. 1992. *Sexual Harassment in Employment Law*. Washington: Press.

Lipka, Susanne, and Elvira Niesner. 1988. Ueber die Arbeit der Agisra gegen Sextourismus und Frauenhandel. *Beigträge zur feministischen Theorie und Praxis* 23: 123–127.

Lodge, Juliet, ed. 1993. *The European Community and the Challenge of the Future*. New York: St Martin's Press.

Lorber, Judith. 1988. In Vitro Fertilization and Gender Politics. In *Embryos, Ethics and Women's Rights: Exploring the New Reproductive Technologies*, ed. E. Hoffmann Baruck et. al., 117–133. New York: Harrington Park.

MacKinnon, Catharine A. 1979. *Sexual Harassment of Working Women: a Case of Sex Discrimination*. New Haven: Yale University Press.

_____. 1983. Feminism, Marxism, Method and the State: Toward Feminist Jurisprudence. *Signs* 8 (4): 635–658.

_____. 1987. *Feminism Unmodified*. Cambridge, Massachusetts: Harvard University Press.

_____. 1989. *Toward a Feminist Theory of the State*. Cambridge, Massachusetts: Harvard University Press.

_____. 1991. Reflections on Sex Equality under Law. *Yale Law Journal* (100): 1281–1328.

_____. 1993. *Only Words*. Cambridge, Massachusetts: Harvard University Press.

Majone, Giandromenico. 1993. The European Community Between Social Policy and Social Regulation. *Journal of Common Market Studies* 31 (2): 153–170.

Malamuth, Neil M., and James V.P. Check. 1983. Sexual Arousal to Rape Depictions: Individual Differences. *Journal of Abnormal Psychology* 92 (1): 55–67.

Mama, Amina. 1989. *The Hidden Struggle: Statutory and Voluntary Sector Responses to Violence Against Black Women in the Home.* London: Runnymede Trust.

Maurer, Mechtilde. 1991. Tourism, Prostitution, AIDS. Paper presented to Seminar on Action Against Traffic in Women, 25–27 September. Strasbourg: Council of Europe. EG/PROST (91).

Mayall, Alice, and Diana E. H. Russell. 1993. Racism in Pornography. In *Making Violence Sexy: Feminist Views on Pornography,* ed. Diana E. H. Russell, 167–179. Milton Keynes: Open University Press.

Mazey, Sonia. 1988. European Community Action on Behalf of Women: The Limits of Legislation. *Journal of Common Market Studies* XXVII (1): 63–84.

Mazur, Amy. 1993. The Formation of Sexual Harassment Policy in France: Another Case of French Exceptionalism? *French Politics and Society* 11 (2): 11–32.

_____. 1996. *Gender Bias and the State: Symbolic Reform at Work in Fifth Republic France.* Pittsburgh: University of Pittsburgh Press.

McCafferty, Nell. 1985. *A Woman to Blame: The Kerry Babies Case.* Dublin: Attic Press.

McCrudden, C. 1991. Between Legality and Reality: The Implementation of Equal Pay for Work of Equal Value in Great Britain. *International Review of Comparative Public Policy* 3: 177–217.

McDonagh, Sunniva, ed. 1993. *The Attorney General v. X and Others. Judgements of the High Court and Supreme Court. Legal Submissions Made to the Supreme Court.* Dublin: Incorporated Council of Law Reporting for Ireland.

McGinley, Gerald P. 1986. Judicial Approaches to Sex Discrimination in the United States and the United Kingdom: A Comparative Study. *Modern Law Review* 49 (4): 413–445.

McNeil, Maureen. 1991. Putting the Alton Bill in Context. In *Off-Centre: Feminism and Cultural Studies,* ed. S. Franklin, C. Lury, J. Stacey, 149–159. London: Harper Collins.

Meehan, Elizabeth. 1993. *Citizenship and the European Community.* London: Sage

Merchant, Vicki. 1994. *Computer Pornography in Schools.* University of Central Lancashire Research Report.

Miralao, Virginia A., Cellia O. Carlos, and Aida Fulleros Santos. 1990. Women Entertainers in Angeles and Olongapo: A Survey Report. Manila, Philippines: Women's Education, Development, Productivity, and Research Organization (WEDPRO) in cooperation with KALAYAAN.

Mooney, Jayne. 1993. *The Hidden Figure: The North London Domestic Violence Survey.* London: Islington Council.

Morris, Naomi. 1993. Jobless and Broke, Former East Bloc Girls Lured to Prostitution. *San Francisco Chronicle,* 30 September.

Murphy-Lawless, Jo. 1993. Fertility, Bodies and Politics: The Irish Case. *Reproductive Health Matters* 2 (November): 53–64.

Mänsson, Sven-Axel. 1992. Brothel "Europe": International Prostitution and Traffic in Women. Unpublished manuscript, Department of Social Work, University of Gothenburg, Sweden.

New York Times. 1994. Rules Sought on Fertilization, 7 January.

_____. 1994. Sexual Harassment Rife in Russia's New Climate, 17 April.

_____. 1994. The Boss Only Wants What's Best for You, 8 May.

Newman, Christine. 1994. Court Says Homes Bill would be an Impossible Invasion into Authority of the Family. *The Irish Times,* 25 January.

O'Connor, Anne. 1985. Listening to Tradition. In *Personally Speaking: Women's Thoughts on Women's Issues,* ed. L. Steiner-Scott, 74–92. Dublin: Attic Press.

Office of Women's Rights. 1993. *Journée Harcèlement Sexuel, 22 juin 1993.* Paris.

Olsen, Frances E. 1989. The Supreme Court 1988 Term—Comment: Unraveling Compromise. *Harvard Law Review* 103 (43): 105–135.

OPCS (Office of Population, Census and Surveys). 1993. *1991 Census Ethnic Group and Country of Birth, Great Britain, Scotland,* Government Statistical Service, CEN91TM EGCB, November.

O'Reilly, Emily. 1991. *Masterminds of the Right.* Dublin: Attic Press.

Outshoorn, Joyce. 1988. Abortion Law Reform: A Woman's Right to Choose? In *Women, Equality and Europe,* ed. Mary Buckley and Malcolm Anderson, 204–219. London: MacMillan Press.

Parlement Européen. 1994. *Combattre le harcèlement sexuel sur les lieux de travail: L'action menée dans les états membres de la communauté européenne.* Luxembourg.

Phillips, Andrew. 1993. Porn from the Skies. *Maclean's* 106: 48.

Picardie, John. 1993. Man on Top. *Independent,* 15 September.

Pillinger, Jane. 1992. *Feminising the Market—Women's Pay and Employment in the European Community.* London: Macmillan.

Police Federation. 1993. *Evidence to Home Affairs Committee on Computer Pornography,* October.

Pornografi: Verklighet eller Fantasi? 1991. Stockholm: Williamsons.

Pornography: Report of the Ministerial Committee of Inquiry. 1989. New Zealand.

Praden, Gauri. Undated. The Road to Bombay: Forgotten Women. In *Red Light Traffic: The Trade in Nepali Girls,* 33–40. Kathmandu, Nepal: ABC/Nepal, a Nepali Women's NGO Working Against Girl Trafficking and AIDS.

Prechal, Sacha, and Noreen Burrows. 1990. *Gender Discrimination Law of the European Community.* Aldershot: Dartmouth Publishing Company.

Prendiville, Patricia. 1988. Divorce in Ireland: An Analysis of the Referendum to Amend the Constitution, June 1986. *Women's Studies International Forum* 11 (4): 355–363.

Pryce Roy, ed. 1987. *The Dynamics of European Union.* Croom Helm: London.

Radford, Jill, and Diana E. H. Russell. 1992. *Femicide: The Politics of Woman Killing.* Milton Keynes: Open University Press.

Randall, Vicki. 1992. The Politics of Abortion: Ireland in Comparative Perspective. *Canadian Journal of Irish Studies* 18 (1): 121–128.

Raymond, Janice G. 1993. *Women As Wombs: Reproductive Technologies and the Battle over Women's Freedom.* New York: HarperCollins.

Reid, Madeleine. 1992. Abortion Law in Ireland after the Maastricht Referendum. In *The Abortion Papers: Ireland,* ed. Ailbhe Smyth, 25–39. Dublin: Attic Press.

Report of the Joint Select Committee on Video Material, Volume 1 and 2. 1988. Australia.

Rhode, Deborah. 1989. *Justice and Gender: Sex Discrimination and the Law.* Cambridge, Massachusetts: Harvard University Press.

Rimmel, Lesley. 1993. Poverty and the Sex Industry Recruit Russian Women. *Women Against Pornography Newsreport* 10 (1).

Robertson, Geoffrey. 1979. *Obscenity: An Account of Censorship Laws and their Enforcement in England and Wales.* London: Wiedenfeld & Nicholson.

Rowland, Robyn. 1987. Of Women Born, But for How Long? The Relationship of Women to the New Reproductive Technologies and the Issue of Choice. In *Made to Order: The Myth of Reproductive and Genetic Progress,* ed. Patricia Spallone and Deborah Lynn Steinberg, 67–83. Oxford: Pergamon Press.

Rubenstein, Michael. 1988. *The Dignity of Women at Work: A Report on the Problem of Sexual Harassment in the Member States of the European Communities.* Brussels: Office for Official Publications of the European Communities.

_____. 1992a. *Preventing and Remedying Sexual Harassment at Work: A Resource Manual.* London: Industrial Relation Services.

_____. 1992b. Sexual Harassment Recommendation and Code. *Equal Opportunities Review* 41: 27–29.

Russell, Diana E. H., and Nicole Van de Van, eds. 1976. *Crimes Against Women: Proceedings of the International Tribunal,* Millbrae, CA: Les Femmes.

Russell, Diana E. H. 1988. Pornography and Rape: A Causal Model. *Political Psychology* 9 (1): 41–73.

_____. 1993a. *Against Pornography: The Evidence of Harm.* Berkeley: Russell Publications.

_____. 1993b. *Making Violence Sexy: Feminist Views on Pornography.* Milton Keynes: Open University Press.

Saylan, Turkan. Prevention of the Causes of Traffic in Women. Paper presented to Seminar on Action Against Traffic in Women, 25–27 September. Strasbourg: Council of Europe. EG/PROST (91).

Sbragia, Alberta M., ed. 1992. *Euro-Politics: Institutions and Policymaking in the "New" European Community.* Washington, D.C.: The Brookings Institute.

Serusclat, Franck M. 1992. *Rapport fait au nom de la commission des Affaires Sociales sur le projet de loi relatif à l'abus d'autorité en matière sexuelle dans les relations de travail et modifiant le code du travail et le code de procédure pénale.* Sénat. no. 350.

Simons, Marlise. 1993. East Europeans Duped into West's Sex Trade. *New York Times,* 9 June.

Smith, Lorna. 1989. *Domestic Violence: An overview of the Literature.* Home Office Research Study 107, London: HMSO.

Smyth, Ailbhe, ed. 1992. *The Abortion Papers: Ireland.* Dublin: Attic Press.

_____. 1992a. "A Great Day for the Women of Ireland": The Meaning of Mary Robinson's Presidency for Irish Women. *Canadian Journal of Irish Studies* 18 (1): 61–75.

_____. 1992b. The Politics of Abortion in a Police State. In *The Abortion Papers: Ireland,* ed. Ailbhe Smyth, 138–148. Dublin: Attic Press.

_____. 1993. The Contemporary Women's Movement in the Republic of Ireland 1970–1990. In *Irish Women's Studies Reader,* ed. Ailbhe Smyth, 245–269. Dublin: Attic Press.

_____. Forthcoming. Haystacks in my Mind, or How to Stay SAFE (Sane, Angry and Feminist) in the 1990s. In *Feminist Activism in the 1990s,* ed. G. Griffin. London: Taylor and Francis.

Squires, Nick. 1993. Behind the Bedroom Door. *Daily Telegraph,* 30 July.

Strategies for the Elimination of Violence Against Women in Society: the Media and Other Means. 1993. Memorandum presented by the Swiss Delegation to the Third European Ministerial Conference on Equality Between Women and Men, 21–22 October, in Rome. Strasbourg: Council of Europe.

Sunstein, Cass. 1992. Neutrality in Constitutional Law (With Special Reference to Pornography, Abortion, and Surrogacy). *Columbia Law Review* 92 (1): 1–52.

Sutton, Jo. 1977–78. The Growth of the British Movement for Battered Women. *Victimology: An International Journal* 2 (3): 576–584.

Tatchell, Peter. 1992. *Europe in the Pink: Lesbian and Gay Equality in the New Europe.* London: GMP Publishers.

Tice, Carol. 1992. Love for Sale. *Utne Reader* (January/February): 38.

United Nations. 1985. *Victims of Crime: The Situation of Women as Victims of Crime, Report of the Secretary-General,* Seventh United Nations Congress on the Prevention of Crime and the Treatment of Offenders, 26 August–6 September, in Milan, Italy. V85–26535 2214T, May.

United Nations. 1993a. *Strategies for Confronting Domestic Violence: A Resource Manual,* United Nations Office at Vienna, Centre for Social Development and Humanitarian Affairs, ST/CSDHA/20, V.93–82831, June.

United Nations. 1993b. *World Conference on Human Rights: The Vienna Declaration and Programme of Action June 1993,* United Nations Reproduction Section, New York, OPI 1394–39399, August 1993–20M.

Van Dijk, P., and G. J. H. Van Hoof. 1990. *Theory and Practice of the European Convention on Human Rights.* 2nd. ed. Deventer-Boston: Kluwer.

Warrior, Betsy. 1976. *Working on Wife Abuse.* Cambridge, Massachusetts: Besty Warrior, 46 Pleasant Street, 02139.

Waxman, Sharon. 1993. "The Newest Profession," *The Washington Post,* 8 September.

West, Lois. 1992. Feminist National Social Movements: Beyond Universalism and Towards a Gendered Cultural Relativism. *Women's Studies International Forum* 15 (5–6): 563–581.

Whelan, Christopher, ed. 1994. *Values and Social Change in Ireland.* Dublin: Gill and Macmillan.

Whitty, Noel. 1993. Law and the Regulation of Reproduction in Ireland: 1922–1992. *University of Toronto Law Journal* 43: 851–888.

Williams, Bernard. 1981. *Obscenity and Film Censorship: An Abridgement of the Williams Report.* Cambridge: Cambridge University Press.

Williams Committee Report. 1979. *Report of the Committee on Obscenity and Film Censorship.* London: HMSO.

Winter, Regine, ed. 1994. *Frauen verdienen mehr. Zur Neubewertung von Frauenarbeit im Tarifsystem.* Berlin: Bund.

Women's Rights Committee. 1994. Report of the Community on Women's Rights on a new post of confidential counsellor at the workplan. PE 204.884/Fin, 27 January: 12.

Won, Kim Hae. 1988. The Realities of Kisaeng Tourism in Cheju Island. In *Exploitation of Women and Children: Its Causes and Effects,* 146–156. Report of Asian Regional Conference, organized by the International Abolitionist Federation in collaboration with Association for Social Health in India, Joint Women's Programme, and Indian Health Organization, 17–19 November. New Delhi: India.

Wyre, Ray. 1992. Pornography and Sexual Violence: Working with Sex Offenders. In *Pornography: Women, Violence and Civil Liberties,* ed. Catherine Itzin, 236–248. Oxford: Oxford University Press.

Zelensky, Anne, and Marie Gaussot. 1986. *Le harcèlement sexuel scandales et réalités.* Paris: Garancière.

Zillmann, Dolf, and James Weaver. 1989. Pornography and Men's Sexual Callousness Towards Women. In *Pornography: Research Advances and Policy Considerations,* ed. Dolf Zillmann and Jennings Bryant, 95–125. Hillsdale, New Jersey: Erlbaum.

CITED CASES

Adoui and Cornuaille v. Belgian State Joined Cases 115 and 116/81 [1982] 3 CMLR 631.

American Booksellers Inc v. William H. Hudnut 771 F.2d 323, 328029 (7th civ. 1985).

Bilka-Kaufhaus GmbH v. Weber Von Hartz Case 170/84 [1986] ECR 1607.

Butler v. Regina (1991), 2. W.W.R. 557.

Chappell v. United Kingdom ECHR, A No. 152, 30 March 1989.

Conegate Limited v. H.M. Customs & Excise Case 121/85; Judgment of 11 March 1986.

Consumer Ombudsman v. Jegerhallen and Olav Thon Case 10/81 Markedsradet (Norwegian Marketing Court) [1982] ECC 335, 9 October 1981.

Defrenne v. Sabena I Case 43/75 [1976] ECR 455; [1976] 2 CMLR 98.

Dekker v. Stichting Vormingscentrum Voor Jonge Volwassen Plus Case 177/88 [1991] IRLR 27.

Grimaldi v. Fonds de Maladies Professionnelles Case 322/88 [1990] IRLR 400.

Grogan v. Society for the Protection of the Unborn Child Case C-159/90 [1990] 3 CMLR 849.

Handyside Case Judgment of 7 December 1976, Series A., No. 24, 1 EHHR 737.

Hertz Case 179/88 [1990] ECR 3879.

Hofmann v. Barmer Ersatzkasse Case 184/83 [1984] ECR 3047.

Integrity Case 373/89 [1991] IRLR 176.

M. v. Crescent Garage Ltd. IT Case No. 23/83 SD.

Müller and others v. Switzerland 24 May 1988, Series A., No. 133, 13 EHRR 212 .

New York v. Ferber 458 U.S. 747 (1982).

Open Door Counseling and Dublin Well Woman v. Ireland (Series A., No. 246) [1992] 15 EHRR 244, 29 October 1992.

Quietlynn and Richards v. Southbend Borough Council Case 23/89; Judgement of 11 July 1990.

Razzouk and Beydoun v. Commission Cases 75 and 117/82 [1984] ECR 1509.

Re A Belgian Prostitute, The Queen of the Netherlands in Council, [1976] 2 CMLR 527, 7 January 1975.

Regina v. Henn and Darby Case 34/79 [1979] ECR 3795.

Robinson v. Jacksonville Shipyards, Inc. 760 F. Supp. 1468 (M.D. Fla. 1991).

The Law Society of British Columbia v. Andrews [1989] 1.S.C.R. 143.

Thoreson v. Guccione No. 13039/81 (N.Y. County, 1990).

x. v. UK [1981] 5 EHRR 501.

x. and y. v. Netherlands (Series A., No. 91) [1986] EHRR 235, 26 March 1985.

NOTES ON CONTRIBUTORS

SUSANNE BAER completed her studies in law and political science at the Free University Berlin with the First Staatsexamen and took the Second Staatsexamen (Bar) in 1991. In 1993, she received her LL.M. from the University of Michigan Law School. She is currently a Doctoral Candidate at the University of Frankfurt am Main and teaches at the Humboldt-University of Berlin.

EVELYN COLLINS has worked on equal opportunities issues since 1982, when she joined the Equal Opportunities Commission for Northern Ireland, a public body with responsibility to eliminate sex discrimination and promote equal opportunities for women and men. She is now its Chief Equality Officer. In March 1992, Evelyn completed a two year secondment to the Equal Opportunities Unit of the European Commission in Brussels, where she was responsible for a range of employment equality initiatives.

CHRISTINE DELPHY is a full-time researcher in Sociology at the French "National Center for Scientific Research" and has worked on feminist analyses of marriage, the family, gender, and related issues for the past twenty-five years. She is the editor of the only national Women's Studies journal in France: *Nouvelles Questions Féministes*, co-founded with Simone de Beauvoir in 1981. She also published *Questions féministes* in 1977 with Simone de Beauvoir. In addition, she is the author of several books, among them *Close to Home* (University of Massachusetts Press 1984), and *Familiar Exploitation: a new analysis of Marriage and the Family in Contemporary Western Societies*, with Diana Leonard (Polity Press 1992).

R. AMY ELMAN is currently Associate Co-director of the Center for European Studies and was formerly Director of the Women's Studies Program at Kalamazoo College where she teaches in the Political Science Department. She has published on Swedish politics and contemporary responses to the Holocaust. Her forthcoming book is entitled *Sexual Subordination and State Intervention: Comparing Sweden and the United States* (Berghahn Books 1996).

JALNA HANMER is Professor of Women's Studies and Co-convenor of the Research Unit on Violence, Abuse and Gender Relations at the University of Bradford, England. She researches and publishes primarily on violence against women and the new reproductive technologies. She has authored several books, the most recent of which is *Women, Violence and Crime Prevention: A Community Study in West Yorkshire* (Gower 1993).

CATHERINE HOSKYNS is Senior Lecturer in International Relations and European Studies at Coventry University. She is a member of the European Forum of Left Feminists and of the European Network of Women. She currently holds a Nuffield Foundation Research Fellowship and is writing a book, *Integrating Gender—Women, Law and Politics in the European Union* (forthcoming, Verso 1996).

CATHERINE ITZIN is an Inspector in the Social Services Inspectorate at the Department of Health writing in a personal capacity as Honor Research Fellow in the Violence Abuse and Gender Relations Research Unit, Department of Applied Social Studies at the University of Bradford and is the editor and co-author of *Pornography: Women, Violence and Civil Liberties* (Oxford University Press 1993).

DORCHEN LEIDHOLDT is Director of Sanctuary for Families' Center for Battered Women's Legal Services in New York City and an adjunct professor at City University of New York Law School. She is Co-director of The Coalition Against Trafficking in Women, a non-governmental organization with consultative status to the United Nations Economic and Social Counsel. Together with Janice Raymond, she co-edited *The Sexual Liberals and the Attack on Feminism* (Pergamon Press 1990).

AMY MAZUR is currently an Assistant Professor of Political Science at Washington State University. She will be publishing *Gender Bias and the State: Symbolic Reform at Work in Fifth Republic France* (University of Pittsburgh Press). She is co-edited with Dorothy McBride Stetson *Comparative State Feminism* (Sage Publications). Her research and teaching interests include feminist policy formation in comparative public policy and the politics of France and Western Europe.

AILBHE SMYTH is Director of the Women's Education Research and Resource Centre at University College, Dublin. She is co-editor of the journal *Women's Studies International Forum* and serves on the editorial boards of several other international journals. Her most recent publications include *Women and Politics in the EC* (Attic Press 1992); *The Abortion Papers: Ireland* (Attic Press 1992); and *The Irish Women's Studies Reader* (Attic Press 1993). Over the years, Ailbhe Smyth has been a member of or consultant to various government and state-sponsored committees, including a five-year term as a member of the Higher Education Authority.

UTE WINKLER is Lecturer of Philosophy at the University of Klagenfurt, Austria. She serves as Director of the Feminist Women's Health Center in Frankfurt, Germany, and is an International Coordinator for the Feminist International Network of Resistance to Reproductive and Genetic Engineering (FINRAGE).

INDEX

abortion, 8
European policy concerning,
11–12, 102, 111, 115, 118,
126–129
in France, 154–155
in Germany, 103
in Ireland, 11–12, 110–111,
116–121
in the Netherlands, 154–155
in Spain, 154–155
UK 1967 Abortion Act, 121
See also European Court of Justice
concerning; Maastricht Protocol; "X" Case
Action Programs, EU, 5, 19, 24, 25
*Adoui and Cornuaille v. Belgian
State,* 92
agriculture, 4
AIDS, 86, 122
Alliance for Choice (Ireland), 124–125
*American Booksellers Inc. v. William H.
Hudnut,* 72
Amnesty International, 70
amniocentesis, 98, 98n.4, 103–
104, 106
Anderson, Malcolm, 1n
André, Michèle, 41–42
anti-Semitism, 69–70
Article 119. *See* Treaty of Rome
Association Européenne Contre Les
Violences Faites aux Femmes
au Travail (AVFT), 28, 38,
41–42, 44, 47

battery, 8, 12, 67
See also violence against women
*Bilka-Kaufhaus GmbH v. Weber Von
Hartz,* 54n.7
Bosnia, EU policy on, 115n
Braidotti, Rossi, 20

Broadcasting Standards Council
(Britain/BSC), 72, 75
Buckley, Mary, 1n
Butler v. Regina, 55n.9

childcare, 19, 121, 142
chrorionic villi sampling (CVF), 98
citizenship, European, 5, 11, 14n, 78,
120, 126, 128, 129
Coalition Against Trafficking in
Women, 95
See also prostitution and sex
trafficking
Code of Practice on Measures to
Combat Sexual Harassment, 23,
25, 27, 29–32
See also European Commission's
Recommendation on the
Protection of the Dignity of
Women and Men at Work; sex-
ual harassment
Cold War, 4
Comité d'Hygiène de Sécurité et
des Conditions de Travail
(CHSCT), 46
Committee on Women's Rights, 18
Common Market, 4, 14, 53
*Conegate Limited v. H.M. Customs &
Excise,* 59, 59n.23
Confédération Française Démocra-
tique du Travail (CFDT), 41, 47
Conseil Supérieur de l'Egalité Profes-
sionelle (CSEP), 42
*Consumer Ombudsman v. Jegerhallen
and Olav Thon,* 60n.25
contraceptives, 105, 106, 121, 122
Convention Against Sexual Exploita-
tion, 95
See also prostitution; sex trafficking
Convention Against Torture and
Other Cruel, Inhumane or

Degrading Treatment or Punishment (CAT), 77, 139–140n
Convention for the Suppression of the Traffic in Persons and of the Exploitation of the Prostitution of Others, 90
See also prostitution; sex trafficking
Convention on the Elimination of All Forms of Discrimination Against Women (CEDAW), 77, 111
Council for the Status of Women (Ireland), 118
Council of Europe, 6n.12, 90n.9
concerning prostitution and sex trafficking, 90, 93, 95
concerning violence against women, 139
Council of Ministers, 6–7
cultural
boundaries, for women and men, 138
exceptionalism, 156
relativism, 155, 156
specificity, 118, 119, 120, 156
and law, 45, 49, 61–62

Declaration on the Elimination of Violence Against Women, 141
See also violence against women
Defrenne v. Sabena, 16, 19
Defrenne, Gabrielle, 16, 16n.5
Dekker v. Stichting Vormingscentrum Voor Jonge Volwassen Plus, 57n.15
democratic deficit, 7, 127
Depro-Provera, 106
Deputy Ministry of Women's Rights (DMWR/France), 44, 45, 46
directives, EU, 8, 10, 28, 29, 36n.4
on broadcasting (89/552/EEC), 10–11, 75
See also Equality Directives
directorate generals (D-Gs), 7
disabled persons
equal treatment for, 5n.8 (*see also* discrimination)
"geneticization" of, 104
preventing births of, 105, 106, 107
rights movement, 99
sterilization of, 106n.9

discrimination
age, 113
disability, 31
employment, 37, 56, 59, 81
gay, 55 (*see also* lesbians)
pornography as sex discrimination, 51, 56, 59, 60, 64, 72, 81
pregnancy, 24
race, 15, 19–20, 69–70, 81, 87n.5, 134
sex, 10, 39, 52–53, 67, 78, 81 (*see also* Article 119)
See also anti-Semitism and homophobia
divorce, 113–114, 119, 126, 130
domestics, 21
Douste-Bluzy, Philippe, 102
Dublin Well Woman Centre, 123
See also *Open Door Counseling and Dublin Well Woman v. Ireland*
Dworkin, Andrea, 80

economic union, 9n.15, 14, 132
ECU (European Currency), 5
Embryo Protection Law (Germany), 100
enlargement of the EU, 4–6
Equal Opportunities Unit, 7, 18, 19, 41, 46
See also Women's Bureau
equal pay, 1, 9, 15–16, 24, 67, 78
See also Article 119
equality, conceptions of, 1, 14, 25, 54–55, 59, 60–61
Equality Directives, 9, 17, 19, 24, 113n.1
equal pay (75/117/EEC), 9, 17, 24
equal treatment (76/207/EEC), 24, 27
pregnancy rights (92/85/EEC), 19n.8
social security (79/7/EEC), 17–18
working conditions (76/207/EEC), 17–18
Euratom, 4n
European and Monetary Union (EMU), 5n.7
European Coal and Steel Community (ECSC), 3–4
European Commission, 7, 19, 43

concerning equal opportunities, 24
concerning pornography, 57
concerning pregnancy, 19
concerning sexual harassment,
    19, 26, 30, 40, 57, 129, 152
concerning violence against
    women, 26, 129, 142–143
concerning women's studies, 148
European Commission's Recommen-
    dation on the Protection of the
    Dignity of Women and Men at
    Work, 29–32, 36, 43n, 48, 151
    See also Code of Practice on Mea-
    sures to Combat Sexual
    Harassment; sexual harassment
European Community (EC), 1, 5–6,
    9n.15, 13n.2, 65
    See also European Union (EU)
European Convention for the Protec-
    tion of Human Rights and Free-
    doms, 54
European Convention on Human
    Rights (ECHR), 6n.12, 76,
    111, 123n
European Convention on Transna-
    tional Frontier Broadcasting, 76
European Court of Human Rights
    (ECHR), 123n
    concerning abortion, 123
European Court of Justice (ECJ),
    6n.12, 8, 28–29, 55, 76, 128
    concerning abortion, 11, 123
    concerning Article 119, 9, 16, 19
    concerning equal pay, 16
    concerning equal treatment in
    employment, 19
    concerning pornography, 59, 75
    concerning prostitution and sex
    trafficking, 92–93
European Network for Women's
    Rights to Abortion and Contra-
    ception (ENWRAC), 129
European Parliament (EP), 7, 26, 127
    concerning gay and lesbian
    rights, 31
    concerning pornography, 57–58
    concerning prostitution and
    trafficking, 90–91
    concerning sexual harassment, 26,
    31, 33

concerning violence against
    women, 90, 139, 139n.5
    women in, 18
European unification, 1, 147

fascism, 104
feminist
    perspective defined, 3n.3
    policy defined, 39n.11
fertility treatments, 106, 106n.8, 107
    See also infertility treatments
Fourth World Conference on
    Women (UN), 141

Gisserot, Hélène, 40
Government's Matrimonial Homes
    Bill (Ireland), 114
*Grimaldi v. Fonds de Maladies Profes-
    sionnelles*, 28–29
*Grogan v. Society for the Protection of
    the Unborn Child*, 123, 127

Handen Thus (Netherlands), 28
Handyside, 59
Hertz, 54n.7
heterosexuals
    and reproductive technologies,
    100, 102
    as implicit legal norm, 55n.8
Hofmann v. Barmer Ersatzkasse, 54n.7
Holocaust, 56, 70
homophobia, 64, 114
homosexuals, 114, 115.
    See also International Lesbian
    and Gay Association
    (ILGA); lesbians

identity politics, 3
immigrants, 21, 64, 84, 89,
    106n.9, 137
in vitro fertilization (IVF), 98
infanticide, 109–110, 120
infertility treatments, 99, 100, 101,
    105, 106–107
    See also fertility treatments
insemination, 100, 101
Integrity, 54n.7
International Council of Women, 95
International Covenant on Civil and
    Political Rights, 77

International Federation for Human Rights, 95
International Tribunal on Crimes Against Women, 133
Irish Women's Liberation Movement (IWLM), 112
Irishwomen United, 112

lesbians, 31, 101, 113
Ligue du Droit des Femme (LDF), 38–39, 40, 41
Lodge, Juliet, 6n.11

M. v. Crescent Garage Ltd., 26
Maastricht Treaty (Treaty on European Union), 5, 9, 11, 111, 127, 142
  French attitude toward, 148
  Protocol (on abortion), 11, 111, 118, 124, 127
  ratification of, 110–111
  referendum, 124–125
  Scandinavian opposition to, 22
MacKinnon, Catharine, 36n.5, 42n.14, 55, 69, 80
Member States, 4–6
Merger Treaty, 4
micro-injections, 100
Ministry of Women's Rights (MWR/France), 39, 40, 42
Mouvement de Libération des Femmes (MLF), 37
Müller and others v. Switzerland, 59n.24

National Alliance of Women's Organizations (NAWO/UK), 80
Neiertz, Véronique, 35n.3, 43–45, 48
loi Neiertz, 46
New York v. Ferber, 56n
Norplant, 106
nuclear energy, 4

Obscene Publications Act (1959/UK), 73, 75, 79
Obscene Publications Branch, 68, 73
obscenity, defined, 73
O'Connor, Anne, 109
Offenses Against the Person's Act (Ireland), 110, 122
Office of Women's Rights (France), 47

Open Door Counseling and Dublin Well Woman v. Ireland, 55n.8
Organization for Economic Development and Cooperation (OECD), 5n.7
Outshoorn, Joyce, 102

part-time workers, 19, 24, 67, 142
parties, political, 61
  in Britain concerning pornography, 71
  in France concerning sexual harassment, 41, 44
  in Germany concerning reproductive technologies, 99, 100–101
Pope John Paul II, 119
pornography, 8, 10, 51
  child, 56n, 58n.20
  computer-generated, 74
  defined, 72, 80
  in the U.S., 55, 70
  Member States on, 58
  sales in Britain, 70
  See also discrimination, pornography as; European Commission concerning; European Court of Justice concerning; European Parliament concerning
pre-implantation diagnosis, 98
prostitution, 11, 58n.19, 77, 78, 83
  dimensions of, 86–89
  Member States on, 93
  physical consequences of, 86
  See also Council of Europe concerning; European Court of Justice concerning; European Parliament concerning; sex trafficking
Public Order Act (UK), 78

Quietlynn and Richards v. Southbend Borough Council, 59n. 23

Race Relations Act (UK), 78, 79
racism. *See* discrimination, race
Randall, Vicki, 128
rape, 2, 8, 55, 55n.8
  in Britain, 68
  in France, 133, 149–150
  in Ireland, 113, 125
Raymond, Jan, 101n

Razzouk and Beydoun v. Commission
  Cases, 54n.6
*Re A Belgian Prostitute, The Queen of
  the Netherlands in Council,*
  92n.12
recommendations, 8, 28–29, 36n.4
Regina v. Henn and Darby, 59n.23
regulations, 8, 36n.4, 28, 102
reproductive technologies, 8, 11
  European-wide policy concerning,
    102, 107
  in Australia, 106
  in England, 101
  in France, 101
  in Germany, 99–101
  in India, 106
  in Italy, 101
  in Sweden, 101
  in the Netherlands, 101
  in the "Third World," 107n
  in the U.S., 101, 106
reproductive tourism, 11, 97
  defined, 101
Resolution on the Exploitation of
  Prostitution and the Traffic in
  Human Beings, 91
Resolution on Violence Against
  Women, 90
Resolution on Violence in the
  Family, 139
Robinson, Mary, 111
Robinson v. Jacksonville Shipyards, Inc.,
  51n.2, 55
Roudy, Yvette, 35n.3, 39, 43, 44

Sbragia, Alberta, 6n.11
Schengen Accord, 84
Schuman Plan, 3n.5, 6n.10
Second World War, 4
  See also WWII
sexual harassment, 8, 9, 23, 151, 152
  defined, 29, 36n.5, 37, 51
  discovery as an issue for EU,
    27–28, 56
  efforts to end in
    Belgium, 32
    Denmark, 32
    France, 9–10, 32, 35n.3, 37,
      44–47, 57, 151–153
    Germany, 57

Ireland, 27, 32
Netherlands, 32
Northern Ireland, 26
Spain, 32
Sweden, 56
U.S., 25, 153
See also European Commission's
  Recommendation on the Pro-
  tection of Dignity of Women
  and Men at Work; Code of
  Practice on Measures to Com-
  bat Sexual Harassment
sex trafficking, 11, 58
  defined, 83
  dimensions of, 86–89
  "Dutch position" concerning, 93
  See also Council of Europe con-
    cerning; European Court
    of Justice concerning
sexual violence, 52
  See also battery; pornography;
    prostitution; rape
Single European Act (SEA), 5
single European currency (ECU), 5
Social Action Programs. *See*
  Action Programs, EU
Social Charter, 5
social policy, 23, 127, 142–143
subsidiarity principle, 9

*The Law Society of British Columbia v.
  Andrews,* 55n.9
Thoreson v. Guccione, 53n.3
trade unions, 18, 20
  concerning reproductive technolo-
    gies (in Germany), 99
  concerning sexual harassment, 26,
    27–28, 43
Treaty of Rome, 1, 4, 15, 24, 127
  Article 119, 1, 9, 15, 16, 24, 54
Treaty on European Union, 5, 7,
  13n.2, 14n
  See also Maastricht Treaty

unemployment in
  East Germany, 99
  Europe generally, 18, 142, 148
  Ireland, 113
  Russia, 88
United Nations (UN), 76–78, 111,
  141, 144

Universal Declaration of Human
    Rights, 76, 139

Veil, Simone, 102
violence against women, 12, 14, 25,
    131, 154
    United Nations concerning, 141
    various states concerning, 133
    Women's Rights Committee
        concerning, 26
    See also battery; sexual violence

West, Lois, 155, 157
Williams Committee on Obscenity
    and Film Censorship (UK), 72

Women Against Sexual Harassment
    (WASH/Britain), 28
Women's Bureau, 7, 18
    See also Equal Opportunities Unit
Women's Rights Committee, 7, 26,
    33, 139, 144
World Conference on Human Rights,
    139–140
World War II, 56
    See also Second World War

"X" Case, 110–111, 117, 118,
    121, 126
x. v. UK, 55n.8
x. and y. v. Netherlands, 55n.8

SEXUAL SUBORDINATION AND STATE INTERVENTION
Comparing Sweden and the United States

R. Amy Elman

One would expect a welfare state such as Sweden to compare favorably with the United States regarding the implementation of public policies and programs. Surprisingly, the author comes to quite different conclusions: in studying the treatment of battered, raped and sexually-harassed women in the two countries, she has found that, contrary to conventional expectation, the ability of the decentralized American state to innovate effectively has been consistently underestimated, whereas Sweden's ability to do the same has often been exaggerated. One explanation seems to be that the very structure of Sweden's centralized, corporatist state does not permit women to make claims on it that do not directly relate to work-force participation. By contrast, the American state is more permeable to the interests of women (as women) in instances where those interests are not economically determined.

By focusing on issues specific to women, this study transcends the emphasis on class which is the traditional basis for social reforms and discussions of the state. Thus, it establishes a more comprehensive comparative political perspective than those presently offered by political analysts concerned with public policy and state structure.

R. Amy Elman is Assistant Professor of Political Science at Kalamazoo College, Michigan, where she also serves as the Director of the Women's Studies Program and as Associate Co-Director of the Center for European Studies.

February 1996, ca. 128 pages, bibliog., index
ISBN 1-57181-071-4, hardback, ca. $35.00/£25.00
ISBN 1-57181-072-2, paperback, ca. $14.50/£10.50

Berghahn Books
165 Taber Avenue, Providence, RI 02906
Phone: 401-861-9330   Fax: 401-521-0046   E Mail: BerghahnBk@aol.com

EUROPE AFTER MAASTRICHT
American and European Perspectives

Edited by Paul Michael Lützeler

During the era following the Second World War world peace was largely assured through American-European cooperation on the political, military, and economic level. This status quo was upset by the ratification of the Treaty on the European Union (Maastricht Treaty) which will, whatever obstacles still remain, inevitably lead to closer cooperation among (west) European countries and to a shift in Europe's position within world politics. This raises a number of questions that are discussed in this volume by an international team of experts from Europe (east and west), Russia and the United States.

Paul Michael Lützeler is Rosa May Distinguished University Professor in the Humanities at Washington University of St Louis; Director of the European Studies Program; Director of the Center for Contemporary German Literature and Chairman of the Senate Council. His most recent publication is *Die Schriftsteller und Europa. Von der Romantik bis zur Gegenwart* (1992)

320 pages, 10 tabl., bibliog., index
ISBN 1-57181-020-X, hardback, $29.95/£23.00

Berghahn Books
165 Taber Avenue, Providence, RI 02906
Phone: 401-861-9330   Fax: 401-521-0046   E Mail: BerghahnBk@aol.com

INTERNATIONAL POLITICAL CURRENTS

A Friedrich-Ebert-Stiftung Series
General Editor: Dieter Dettke

Volume 1:
TOWARD A GLOBAL CIVIL SOCIETY

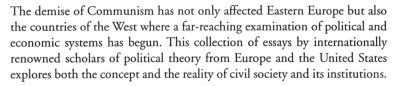

Edited by Michael Walzer

The demise of Communism has not only affected Eastern Europe but also the countries of the West where a far-reaching examination of political and economic systems has begun. This collection of essays by internationally renowned scholars of political theory from Europe and the United States explores both the concept and the reality of civil society and its institutions.

Michael Walzer has been a permanent faculty member at the School of Social Science, Institute for Advances Study in Princeton since 1980. He is an editor of *Dissent* and a contributing editor of *The New Republic,* and has published among numerous works *The Company of Critics* (1988) and *Interpretation and Social Criticism* (1987).

344 pages, ISBN 1-57181-054-4, hardback
$39.95/£31.00

Volume 2:
UNIVERSITIES IN THE TWENTY-FIRST CENTURY

Edited by **Steven Muller,** Chairman of the Twenty-first Century Foundation

On the eve of the twenty-first century, the United States and Germany face common but also separate challenges that will be met in part by significant activity at the university level. This volume offers views and expert opinions from leading American and German educators and university administrators on the future role of this vital educational and cultural institution in both societies.

192 pages, ISBN 1-57181-026-9, hardback
ca. $29.95/£22.00

Berghahn Books

165 Taber Avenue, Providence, RI 02906
Phone: 401-861-9330   Fax: 401-521-0046   E Mail: BerghahnBk@aol.com

EDUCATION FOR THE NEW EUROPE

Edited by **Dietrich Benner** and **Dieter Lenzen**

Up to now European unification has primarily been considered a matter of political and economic concern. Very little attention has been paid to education and training, although many resolutions of the various treaties, especially regarding the labor market, would remain ineffectual without any synchronization of the various systems of education and training. Moreover, if popular support for political and economic integration is to be secured, the citizens of Europe, in Delors' words, must "genuinely have the feeling that they are involved in this joint adventure (Europe)," which will be achieved only through a better understanding of each other's history and also an awareness of common European history and common cultural traditions. This volume presents a selection of papers given at a recent meeting, attended by representatives from about thirty European countries who had come together to take stock after Maastricht and to develop new perspectives for a future European educational system.

Dietrich Benner is Professor of Education at the Institute of Education, Humboldt University, Berlin; **Dieter Lenzen** is Professor of Education at the Institute of General and Comparative Education, Freie Universität Berlin and President of the German Society for Education.

February 1996, 192 pages, ISBN 1-57181-074-9, hardback
ca. **$29.95/£22.00**

Berghahn Books
165 Taber Avenue, Providence, RI 02906
Phone: 401-861-9330   Fax: 401-521-0046   E Mail: BerghahnBk@aol.com